Clare Mal

Searching
the Pockets

A Poetics of Primary Education

Caroline —
Thanks for comin +
for everything else !!!
Cheers,
Clare

VERITAS

First published 2007 by
Veritas Publications
7/8 Lower Abbey Street
Dublin 1
Ireland
Email publications@veritas.ie
Website www.veritas.ie

ISBN 978 1 85390 843 9

Copyright © Clare Moloney, 2007

10 9 8 7 6 5 4 3 2 1

A catalogue record for this book is available from the British Library.

All poetry and extracts taken from Seamus Heaney's *Preoccupations: Selected Prose 1968–1978* are courtesy of Faber and Faber, 1980. All poetry and extracts taken from Seamus Heaney's *Door into the Dark* are courtesy of Faber and Faber, 1969. All poetry and extracts taken from Seamus Heaney's *Seeing Things* are courtesy of Faber and Faber, 1991. All poetry and extracts taken from *Things Made and Things Said* by Gertrude Patterson are courtesy of the Stranmillis Press, 1999. Lines from Brendan Kennelly's 'Poem from a Three Year Old' (p. 141) are taken from *A Time for Voices: Selected Poems 1960–1990*, courtesy of Bloodaxe Books, 1990. Line from Jan Kochanowski's 'Lament 8' (p. 145) from *Laments*, translated by Seamus Heaney and Stanislaw Baranczak, courtesy of Faber and Faber, 1995. Lines from Ted Hughes' 'The Warm and the Cold' (pp. 201–2) are taken from Pauline Kelly's *Time for Poetry*, courtesy of Folens, 1991. 'Afternoon with Irish Cows' (pp. 220–1) by Billy Collins is taken from *Picnic, Lightning*, courtesy of University of Pittsburg Press, 1998.

Designed by Colette Dower
Cover illustration by Turlough McKevitt
Printed in the Republic of Ireland by Wood Printcraft, Dublin

Veritas books are printed on paper made from the wood pulp of managed forests. For every tree felled, at least one tree is planted, thereby renewing natural resources.

to my parents
and their parents

We have thought too much
in terms of a will which submits
and not enough in terms of an imagination
which opens up
Paul Ricoeur

Contents

Acknowledgements

This work owes a debt of gratitude to many pupils, teachers, colleagues, friends and family members. The pupils of both primary schools in the parish of Stabannon and Kilsaran in the 1990s are adults now; some are young teachers. Their youthful contribution to my understanding of the nature of teaching, learning and poetry's role within it is the heart and soul, not to mention the body and bones, of this book. Along with their contribution, the conversations and encouragement of teaching colleagues and friends in various areas of education – Gertrude Patterson, Alex McEwan, Joe Dunne, Eoin Cassidy, John Devitt, Brendan McDonnell, Maura Hyland, Tom Hamill, Mary O'Flynn – have proved critically creative company within which to ruminate. I wish to thank the editors at Veritas for their patience, persistence and sound editorial sense. They have proved a solid and steady post on which I have leaned heavily. A particular debt of gratitude is owed to Mount Oliver Institute Trust for generous financial assistance while researching this work. But more than that, while many are fortunate in being able to point to the influence of an exceptional teacher in their lives, I regard myself as particularly fortunate in being able to point to an exceptional institute – Mount Oliver Institute, where I spent one of the most deeply educational years of my life. Its influence on me as a teacher cannot be overestimated.

Professional and personal coalesce as I remember with particular fondness my first primary school teacher, my aunt Brigid – another daughter of the Fear Léinn who first introduced me to the whole business of reading and writing. *Gabhaim molta Bríde*. Finally, I acknowledge my family's and in particular my husband Ciaran's support during the very lengthy writing process of this book.

Introduction

Fifteen years ago, while browsing the prospectus of a postgraduate course, I made an impulsive decision. Feeling that I had enlisted in enough of the premier-league subjects of educational studies – Classroom Management, Curriculum Studies, Sociology and Philosophy of Education and so on – I marked myself down for one module entitled 'Approaches to Poetry'. Three months or so later, I drove the streets of Belfast in search of Stranmillis College where the course I had – rashly – chosen was to be held. I arrived late, stressed and with a headache and took my place among a small group of six or seven students as one by one they introduced themselves and explained their choosing of the course. I listened with a mixture of admiration and irritation as each one spoke of their interest in poetry, their attraction to the work of this or that poet, favourite poems, memorable lines and so on. I squirmed, knowing I could not honestly claim any real *love* of poetry. I could not pretend to be a reader of poetry; I did not own a single poetry book; I didn't have a favourite poem. All I could remember was a few lines from Browning's 'My Last Duchess' and Wordsworth's 'The Prelude' which was on our A-Level English course. As a primary teacher too – even though children's poetry had come a long way in terms of the relevance and fun of its subject matter – poetry had not been a priority for me; if I came across a poem in a reading book I might 'do it' and I might not. So, when my turn came to speak I had to admit that the only reason I was present was because a last-minute attempt to ditch my original decision (now most definitely a mistake, I thought) and opt out of the course had backfired. Other courses I sought instead were fully subscribed and so I had no choice but to continue. As I sat there that first night I felt a definite mixture of irritation and resentment at being in this predicament, feelings made all the more raw by the fact that I had no one to blame but myself. Yet as I listened, I also felt a sneaking suspicion that in relation to poetry, my colleagues might be on to something that had so far passed me by. This mixture of feelings precipitated a rather contrary mood. Always ready instinctively to 'trust contrariness'[1] I sat back in my chair, surveying the comments of my colleagues as though they were buns being passed around on a cake stand. In the silence of my detached vantage point, I became aware of the voice of mother-in-me whisper skeptically to my-grandmother-in-me, 'I'd say them's bought buns' to which came the rather withering reply, 'Sure you'd know to look at them'. Obviously my mood ill-disposed me to the comments of my colleagues, but those voices that stirred in me then surfaced – albeit fleetingly – an unconscious, perhaps hereditary *prejudice* towards poetry. (I was reminded again of those voices when I later read in Heaney's *Preoccupations,* 'One half of one's sensibility is in a cast of mind that comes from belonging to a place, an ancestry, a history, a culture, whatever one wants to call it'.)[2] Something in my cast of mind seemed to suspect poetry of being a kind of fancy confectionery; language 'piped' prettily into shape, experience with icing on. While poetry was admirable, it somehow lacked the authenticity of the genuinely hands-on, home-made. The Bull Report into the teaching of English, *A*

Language For Life, might have had me in mind when it commented:

> It has to be acknowledged that poetry starts at something of a disadvantage. In the public view it is something rather odd, certainly outside the current of normal life ...[3]

I sat there that first night, sulking to myself at the thought of having to thole twelve weeks of 'this'. I didn't know then what I know now as I use the word 'sulking'. Deep down within those voices, somewhere between the impulse to 'do' poetry and the unconscious suspicion that it was somehow not true to real life, something fishy was going on. According to the Oxford Universal Dictionary 'sulky' describes 'a fish that remains in hiding and motionless when hooked'. Hiding as I was in my silent skepticism, reluctant to engage with poetry (an experience which was to prove invaluable when I would later meet the same reluctance in my pupils), I was already and without knowing it 'hooked'. Even on that very first night those conflicting voices, feelings and intuitions that surfaced in me were, I realise now, an example of poetry beginning to educate deeply, confirming Brendan Kennelly's belief that: 'Poetry is the deepest education there is, a conscious, structured, logical, inspiring illumination of the various darknesses within us all.'[4]

The reeling-in of that fish happened slowly, over several years, much reflection, many written drafts and many quarrels with myself. It is the development of a story of rash, then reluctant, then begrudging engagement with poetry, to its ultimate end: *this book,* a written response to my growing belief in the importance, not just of poetry but of *poetry as education*; not just of poetry as education but as the kind of depth education that is vital in nourishing life-to-the-full. I too believe that 'Poetry is the deepest kind of education there is'. This book is about that kind of education. It is about education that is interested not just in highly but in *deeply* qualifying its participants, both learners and teachers. And, since both general and religious education have the common aim of nourishing childhood to the full,[5] I concern myself in this book with the role of the poetic in both.

That poetry teaches is not a new idea, but when I began my postgraduate studies neither poetry nor its relationship with education were of particular interest to me. Educational discourse revolved around the languages of those premier-league subjects I mentioned earlier. It was those that received most of my educational attention. Poetry as far as I was concerned was a section in the English curriculum, no more and no less. Now, years later, I recognise the truth of Patrick Kavanagh's caution that a man dabbles in verse and finds it is his life, or Seamus Heaney's description of poetry as 'a dig for finds that end up being plants'.[6] The Czech poet Miroslav Holub once said, 'I like writing for people untouched by poetry; for instance, for those who do not even know that it should be at all for them. I would like them to read poems as naturally as they read the papers, or go to a football game'.[7] This book is written *for* teachers, especially for those teachers who do not consider themselves inclined towards poetry, *by* a teacher who had not considered herself so inclined either.

Despite what I believe to be its deeply educative potential, however, poetry is not written in order to teach. It does not canvas new methodologies, technologies, concepts or practices. Nor, although it is written about education, does this book seek to teach or canvas particular ways of teaching. I write simply to offer an account of how engagement with poetry offers opportunities for exploration that may deeply educate both pupil and teacher. And not just the individual child but also the class and school community of teachers-and-pupils. I write to offer an example of poetry 'as divination, poetry as revelation of the self to the self, as restoration of the culture to itself'.[8] Revelation of the self to the self is a deeply educative process. It sponsors a lifelong exploration of the questions, 'Who am I? Who are we?' and in a postmodern context, 'What is the nature of identity anyway?' I hope to show this exploration happening in the classroom through engagement with poetry and its writing process. I hope to show it happening for both the pupil and teacher because my experience in doing so has brought me beyond 'child-centredness' to a view of the classroom as a space in which pupil and teacher meet in a relationship of educational interdependence. They meet in a space in which teaching and learning are not – or at least not always – discrete activities. Teaching is an oral tradition. The medium of the classroom is language; language is fluid. In it the role of the teacher and the pupil co-mingle like different colours in a watercolour. In this book I hope to show not only poetry's facilitation of the question of identity for the persons and community involved, but also how it 'identifies' teaching and learning and their interdependency.

The question of identity is not confined in this book to the pupil and teacher but includes education's own identity in the present post-industrial, postmodern moment. I hope to show how engagement with poetry may restore *educational culture* to itself. By giving a poetic account of education as I, through poetic texts and images, have come to know it, I will recount what the French philosopher Jean Francois Lyotard might call 'a little narrative'. For Lyotard little narratives need telling in order that whatever is the *Grand Narrative*, or dominant ideology or theory of the day, might be challenged. It seems to me that educational ideology today arises out of a particular version of technical-rationalism in which education plans lessons which set objective aims and then works out a set of methodological steps towards those aims. Success or failure in achieving these aims is subsequently verified by equally objective assessment according to observable criteria. There is of course a place for such theory in education *provided* it is one story among other stories. However, should it come to occupy a place of overarching authority, should it consolidate into the way, the truth and the life of education, then the truth told by stories which offer a different version of education is at risk of being suppressed. By having recourse to poetry I hope to remind education – both general and religious – that it has within its tradition a certain poetic strain as well as a strain with a high degree of 'reasonability'. I hope to tell a story in which education follows the experienced intuition as much as the lesson-plan.

Heaney uses the word 'divination' in the context of water divining as a metaphor for poetry as pure gift rather than acquired craft.[9] But it is no coincidence that it is an apt image in the religious sense too. Speaking about his poem 'The Diviner' Heaney says: 'The diviner resembles the poet in his function of making contact with what lies hidden, and in his ability to make palpable what was sensed or raised.'[10] It is my belief that the diviner resembles the teacher and the religion teacher also. The task of religious education and the role of the poetic within it is the very same as the diviner's task. Its function is to divine 'living water', to make contact with the hidden depths of religious experience, so that from those depths both pupils and teachers may experience that living water 'suddenly broadcasting its secret [or sacred] stations'. The teacher who would teach children about poetry needs to be sensitive to 'the pluck' of experience, to facilitate 'that first stirring of the mind round a word or an image or a memory or a symbol to grow towards articulation'. The religious educator must do the same in terms of that stirring; she must facilitate its growing towards the expression of religious experience. When religious education 'divines' in this way, the water that is released irrigates the life of the individual and the life of his or her community too. The role of poetry and sensitivity to the poetic are vital if religious education is, paradoxically, to 'aspire' to life's deepest possible depths. For me, in terms of religious education, the theologian Amos Niven Wilder summed it up when he said, 'But all this means that the artists and the poets are more important to us than ever before'.[11]

Despite my belligerent beginnings, I continued to explore the role of poetry in education under the working title: *Poetry and Its Writing Process in the English Curriculum of the Primary School*. As a title it didn't work for very long. The Northern Ireland Curriculum notes that, '… poetry needs to be at the heart of work in English because of the quality of language at work on experience which it offers us'.[12] But a hunch insisted that exactly because of *the quality of language at work on experience*, because of the critical role of that work in the learning process, poetry should not be confined to the English curriculum. One of my aims in this book is to exemplify poetry's role in, but also beyond, the English curriculum. I hope to offer evidence that its writing process is as an overarching model of education in itself. I hope to show the depth of learning that can take place when language and experience 'work' on each other. T.S. Eliot once expressed a concern that what we cease to be able to find words for we cease to be able to feel. His concern points to this close relationship between language and experience or, in religious terms, between word and word-made-flesh. Curricula in schools, both in general and in religious education, have emphasised the importance of language for life and for learning. The Bullock Report states that: 'To bring knowledge into being is a formulating process, and language is its ordinary means, whether in speaking or writing or in the inner monologue of thought'.[13] The General Directory on Catechesis likewise states that 'Inculturation of the faith, under certain aspects, is a linguistic task'.[14] In this book, both in relation to general and to religious education, I seek to amplify and exemplify poetry's role in enhancing the quality of work that language and experience 'do' on each other.

In the relationship between language and experience the words 'at work on each other' might well be replaced by one: *'imagination'*. What goes on between language and experience is primarily, I believe, imagination's doing. What is at work between experience and language is essentially *imaginary* by nature. Not that naming the relationship between language and experience as 'imagination' clarifies anything, for it is difficult to be definitive with regard to what exactly imagination is. The philosopher Richard Kearney puts it succinctly when he says, 'there has always been more to imagination than has ever been dreamed of in our philosophies'.[15] It is understandable then why the word 'imagination' is often employed in conversation with more assumptions than explanations as to its meaning. Bearing in mind that the Aramaic word for sin may be translated as 'wide of the mark', my attempt here in relation to children, education and imagination is to be more precise. While as educators we might agree with Picasso that 'Every child is an artist', we have less clarity with regard to ways of working with the problem he went on to identify in the second part of his statement – 'the problem is how to help him to remain so as he grows up'. Initially, as I worked in my classroom with children, imagination, poetry writing and so on, I found myself encouraging children to 'use your imagination' but fairly bereft of specifics in relation to what those words meant, *practically* and *pedagogically*. In an effort to bring the relationship between language, experience and imagination out of the realm of vague if well-intentioned exhortation and place it within general and religious education's grasp and responsibility, this work turns to poetry and its writing process and seeks to make imagination more explicit by examining the processes whereby poetry 'gets made'.

In relation to our tendency to endorse the imaginative in children, James Hillman suggests that, 'Western consciousness with its one-sided extravagances of will and reason ... has abandoned the *mundus imaginalis* to children'.[16] If, as I claim, teaching as an activity is not the preserve of a certain kind of reason-based approach but is also imaginative activity, then abandonment of imagination to children/pupils may lead to a denial of imagination in the adult/teacher. Such a denial will have the effect of crippling her teaching, not to mention her living. For how can we support the aims of both education and religious education to nourish children in living to the full if we as adults, as teachers, cannot begin to *imagine* what that might be like? As Richard Kearney has also said, '... better to appreciate what it means to imagine is, I will argue, better to appreciate what it means to be'.[17] 'Today,' Kearney claims, 'we rely more than ever on the power of imagining to suggest other ways of being in the world, other possibilities of existence, underpinning Ricoeur's view that there is "no action without imagination".'[18] This of course brings such religious concerns as Kingdom, prophecy, justice, the symbolic, ritual etc. directly into the dynamism of that relationship between imagination, language and experience, as much as into the realm of the English, or the verbal arts curriculum. For example, in relation to the central teaching of Jesus – the Kingdom – is the role of imagination not *vital* to the process of entering the Kingdom, particularly if that entry is via the language of story, via parable? Again, Amos Wilder puts it well when he says, 'When imagination fails, doctrines become ossified, witness and proclamation wooden, doxologies and litanies empty, consolations hollow, and ethics legalistic'.[19] To this I would add that a religious education that puts its faith in prescribed methodologies, rather than imagination shrivels. Let me repeat therefore that, in relation to this book, my intense preoccupation with establishing a role for poetry and its writing process 'as a model of education' refers not only to the general curriculum, but also to the religious.

Having spoken of three key dimensions in the learning process – language, experience and imagination, this book also focuses on a fourth member of this close-knit community – tradition. The term tradition often suffers from being thought of as the handing on or transmission of some precious deposit of material from one generation to the next. I favour an understanding of tradition which does not see it as an object, the precious vase being a common image. Rather I view tradition as a kind of historical-cultural subsoil in which the life of the individual and his or her community has its roots and receives vital nourishment. These, like all roots, sustain us even if we are not always conscious of them. Indeed tradition is all the more powerful when we are not conscious of its living influence on our present. In his book *Back To The Rough Ground*, the philosopher Joe Dunne calls tradition in this sense,

> the past as present, all the more present because of its being for the most part pre-reflective, active from behind one as it were, rather than something one can place before oneself as object.[20]

Others have suggested the image of tradition as that which whispers over our shoulder, behind our backs. In the case of the story recounted earlier, tradition finds an aural image in the voices of the mother and grandmother whispering in my ear. Just as I poked and rooted around in poetry and 'unearthed' those voices that very first night, so too as I poked around in the whole business of poetry and education I unearthed different cultural traditions, each with its own distinct voice and prejudice. The word 'education' comes from the word '*educare*', one meaning of which is 'to lead out'. Exploring this image unearthed the voice of Plato speaking from his cave with its slaves heading from its dark interior towards the bright light of the sun, from ignorance to knowledge. In terms of a Celtic poetic educational tradition, however, my explorations led me to the poets assembled at the beginning of the Táin (Kinsella's translation) commissioning their young apprentices to go in search of a vital story which they, the poets, even between them, cannot fully remember. The young poets' search takes them in the opposite direction from Plato's slaves, i.e. not from darkness to light, but from light to darkness. It is in the darkness that 'the whole story' becomes audible. The young apprentice poet returns the story of the Táin to his awaiting community and they rejoice. In terms of the Judeo-Christian educational tradition, I expected to follow the educational direction of the Exodus story from slavery to freedom, but a certain parable confounded my expectations – as parables are wont to do – and I found myself in terms of this religious tradition 'at sea', learning and teaching from the boat. But that is another story and one I will come to in Chapter 3.

These images – of leading out, of darkness and light, of nourishing, of teaching from the boat – are what I believe Carl Jung had in mind when he spoke about 'archetypal images': 'images charged with numinosity or psychic energy which becomes dynamic and from which consequences of some kind must flow.'[21] In this book, with the help of certain pieces of poetry, I engage with these foundational images in an attempt to identify their influence, to guess where their psychic energies flow or are staunched in education today and what the consequences may be for teaching and learning. In doing so I hope to extend the backward reach of our sense of education, so that we may hear it speaking to us and through us, so that we may become aware of its various ancestral endowments.

There are two sections in this book. The first contains three separate chapters that, with the help of poetry, explore three different educational traditions or heritages – Greek, Celtic and Judeo-Christian. Each chapter muses on the inherited traits that ancestry bestows on education today and their influence on the extent to which education fosters the poetic. The second section – five chapters – explores poetry and its practical workings in the classroom, in terms of both general and religious education. By drawing on the work of established poets, in particular Seamus Heaney, and on the classroom work of the teacher and pupils (four to twelve year olds) in Scoil San Nioclás Stabannon and Scoil Mhuire Gan Smál, Kilsaran, 1990–1995, as well as from curriculum statements and reports, I try to make more explicit the process whereby poetry *gets* made. By focusing on the process whereby poetry gets made I want to *make more explicit the kind of learning that is fostered in poetry's writing process* so that it may be valued not just as an important part of the language curriculum but as an overarching model of education and religious education in itself. At the same time I want to offer some children's poems *as poetry in their own right*. Having said that, I must emphasise that this section of the book does not wish to showcase children's poetry like a shop-window display. This is the legitimate aim of other types of publications, for example the McDonald's Young Writers series (*The Bees Knees, The Cat's Pyjamas*, etc.) but it is not mine. Nor do I wish to offer a 'how to' of teaching children poetry writing.

Any experience I have suggests to me that you always approach poetry writing *without* a pre-established methodology and you come out the far end, wiser and more experienced alright, but still without a methodological guarantee of future success. A substantial portion of this work draws on work previously published in a chapter entitled 'In the Saying and the Doing', in Dr Gertrude Patterson's book *Things Made and Things Said*. Here, however, I infuse the detail of how poetry is made with philosophical reflection on the nature of language, learning, experience and imagination. In other words I try to offer evidence in support of my claim that poetry's writing process offers a model of education *per se*.

Education today bears a huge burden. It continues to be focused on as both the *cause* and the *remedy* of many of society's disappointments:

> Teachers more than anyone are expected to build learning communities, create the knowledge society, and develop the capacities for innovation, flexibility and commitment to change that are essential for economic prosperity. At the same time, teachers are also expected to mitigate against and counteract many of the immense problems that knowledge societies create, such as excessive consumerism, loss of community, and widening gaps between rich and poor. Somehow, teachers must try to achieve these seemingly contradictory goals at the same time. This is their professional paradox.[22]

In the face of pressure exerted on education to respond appropriately in this situation, it is at risk of becoming a practical means towards various practical ends, all of which seek ultimately to relieve human anxiety in an increasingly insecure world. I believe that an education that fosters an intimate relationship with language at its most poetic can address this paradox and the anxiety it generates. It can model a way of working creatively with our human condition that does not seek to deny its human vulnerability but works, word for word, to understand it, lament it at times, celebrate it at other times, but ultimately nourish its living to the full.

I wish to acknowledge at this point a dependency on the works of Seamus Heaney and Joseph Dunne. Their works are like main roads that have greatly facilitated my travels through the realms of poetry and education.

Notes

1. Heaney, S., 'Casting and Gathering' in *Seeing Things*, London, Faber and Faber, 1991, p. 13.
2. Heaney, *Preoccupations: Selected Prose*, London, Faber and Faber, 1980, p. 35.
3. *A Language For Life*, The Bullock Report, Report of the Committee of Inquiry appointed by the Secretary of State for Education and Science, London, HMSO, 1975, Chap. 9.22, p. 135.
4. Kennelly, B., *Journey into Joy: Selected Prose,* Ake Persson (ed.), Newcastle-Upon-Tyne, Bloodaxe, 1994, p. 64.
5. Primary School Curriculum Intro. 'to enable the child to live a full life as a child ...', The Stationery Office, 1999, p. 7; *Alive-O* Programme (4): 'The title "Alive-O" reflects one of the overriding aims of religious education, namely, to enable people to become fully alive to the presence of God in themselves, in others and in the world around them.' Dublin, Veritas, 1999, p. vii.
6. *Preoccupations*, p. 41.
7. Cited in Heaney, *The Government of the Tongue*, London, Faber and Faber, 1988, p. 47.
8. *Preoccupations*, p. 41.
9. *The Diviner*
   Cut from the green hedge a forked hazel stick
   That he held tight by the arms of the V:
   Circling the terrain, hunting the pluck
   Of water, nervous, but professionally

Unfussed. The pluck came sharp as a sting.
The rod jerked with precise convulsions,
Spring water suddenly broadcasting
Through a green hazel its secret stations.

The bystanders would ask to have a try.
He handed them the rod without a word.
It lay dead in their grasp till nonchalantly
He gripped expectant wrists. The hazel stirred.
(*Preoccupations*, p. 48).

10. Ibid.
11. Wilder, A.N., 'Art and Theological Meaning' in *The New Orpheus: Essays Toward a Christian Poetic,* Nathan A. Scott, Jr. (ed.) New York, Sheed and Ward, 1964, p. 408.
12. *Proposals for the English Curriculum,* Report of the English Working Group, Belfast, NICC, 1989, Chap. 2, 3.12, p. 14.
13. *A Language for Life*, Chap. 4.9, p. 50.
14. *General Directory on Catechesis*, Part Four, Chap. 5, 'Catechesis in the Socio-Cultural Context: Language', Dublin, Veritas, 1998, p. 215.
15. *Poetics of Imagining: Modern to Postmodern,* New York, Fordham University Press, 1998, p. 57.
16. *The Sociology of Childhood*, Batsford Academic and Educational Ltd., 1982, p. 107.
17. *Poetics of Imagining*, p. 1.
18. Ibid., p. 150.
19. *Theopoetic: Theology and the Religious Imagination*, Lima, Ohio, Academic Renewal Press, 2001, p. 2.
20. *Back To The Rough Ground: 'Phronesis' and 'Techne' in Modern Philosophy and in Aristotle*, Notre Dame, London, University of Notre Dame Press, 1993, p. 359.
21. *Man and his Symbols*, London, Picador, 1964, p. 87.
22. Hargreaves, A., *Teaching in the Knowledge Society: Education in the Age of Insecurity*, p. 9.

1 Into the Light

When I first began to teach I worked energetically and enthusiastically; I liked teaching, in fact I loved it. I thought a lot about what I was doing and how I was doing it. I thought about how, and if, I might need to do it differently; I talked informally with other teachers, gleaning insights in the process; I looked out for practical ideas, gathered resourceful paraphernalia, equipped myself and my classroom. In short I took to it and got happily on with it. The only thorn in my side was this business of doing notes. During my teacher education and probationary years I did them, but in a purely perfunctory sense. That is to say that while I did them, I did not believe in them. Later I likened the doing of notes to writing out the aims and objectives, as well as the menu and ingredients for a week's dinners: in theory something one might usefully do but in reality not how being a mother/wife/housekeeper 'worked'. Once I was safely out of probation, the doing of notes – not to be confused with preparation – fell by the wayside unless some inspection threatened and they had to be resurrected and re-jigged. Even then, several years into my teaching life, notes were things to keep others happy, not something I did for myself. Although I continued to teach without them, the issue of notes nagged at me and raised the suspicion that I was being less than thorough, unprofessional, undisciplined – in short, not teaching properly. For the next ten years or so of my teaching life I carried an undifferentiated, inarticulable resistance towards what I construed as this official mode in which teaching was supposed to be 'done-up and turned-out'. At the same time I harboured a nervousness that how I was doing it – i.e. according to some kind of reasonable process, yes; but deeper than that too, by instinct and ongoing reflection on experience – was somehow amateurish. It was not so much the notes in themselves – some people find a shopping list a useful way of keeping track, some don't – it was the philosophy or approach to teaching that they had come to represent, the idea of teaching as an activity that should conduct itself logically, according to plan. It was as though – well at that time I could only say metaphorically – I was supposed to be teaching according to my right hand when I would have been naturally inclined to use my left or, to change the metaphor, I seemed to continually play my teaching game on an away pitch; never a home game. It was as though something wanted to tie my teaching down to theoretical minutia with Lilliputian threads.

It is significant that these ways of describing the problem are images that come from the realm of the poetic, not from the realm of theory or educational concept. That, I believe, is because behind the issue of notes or lesson plans and their approach to teaching is the deeper issue of language, how education talks about itself and therefore comes to understand itself. In the face of that problem I was like the child who cannot even begin to answer that fairly futile question, 'What is it you don't understand?' I had an instinct that something was amiss but I was unable to put words on a vague hunch especially when, were I to explain what the matter was, I would have to do so in an 'official' educational language I did not speak very well – play another away game – and those to whom I would be explaining did not seem to speak of teaching in ordinary language.

I taught in primary schools for fifteen years before I began to suspect that the key to the issue of how education talks about or theorises itself and, therefore, how education understands itself goes deep into ancient Greek philosophy. Underneath that, it goes even deeper into the subsoil of the relationship between Greek poetry and philosophy. But when I began teaching I had little or no idea that the ancient voices of both whispered behind my back when I entered a college of education as a 'Wilson Grad' in 1977. I assumed education all began – or, more accurately, began properly – with the New Curriculum of 1971 and the *Children of God* series underpinned by the various theories of Piaget, Kohlberg or Fowler and the new educational 'religions' of child-centeredness and discovery learning. I did not know, or care too much, that the very word 'education' came to us from the word *educare* or *educere*, meaning in one sense 'to lead out' and in another sense 'to nourish' or rear young. (In retrospect I should have seen that, even in its etymological roots, education was by nature a two-faced affair.) Nor did I appreciate that language, words in themselves, were much more than just a cluster of letters denoting a definition – the sort of thing that used to provide ammunition for the opening round of fire in our secondary school debates. It took an involvement with poetry to teach me that words are a way in and out of meaning that goes deeper than definition and official discourse; that words are a 'Door Into the Dark' or, in the case of this chapter, into the light. In the words of Seamus Heaney:

> When I called my second book *Door Into the Dark* I intended to gesture towards this idea of poetry as a point of entry into the buried life of the feelings or as a point of exit for it. Words themselves are doors; Janus is to a certain extent their deity, looking back to a ramification of roots and associations and forward to a clarification of sense and meaning.[1]

Once my suspicions about Greek philosophy were aroused[2] I felt a desire to confront Plato, meet him face to face and have it out with him. But where or who was the original Plato? How could I get to him across two thousand years and a mountainous range of scholarly philosophical discourse, without having had the high-altitude language training that would be required to survive such an expedition? And if I did meet him what then? Just knock on his door and say, 'Excuse me Plato ...?' More or less! My attempt in this chapter is to knock on the portal that is the word '*educare*'; to wait and listen imaginatively, poetically, in the hope of hearing some of those ancient voices inviting me to come in and explore the deeper reaches of the Greek educational impulse that throbs in education today. I do so in order that I may equip my ear to pick up the echoes of ancient Greek rhyme, rhythm and reason in the way primary education speaks and behaves today. I do so in order that I might more fully understand what goes on beneath the surface facts-of-the-matter of primary education. I hope to work with the word '*educare*' in such a way that it offers access into the buried life of my own feelings and intuitions about education, intuitions sprung from my experience as a teacher, my experience of some kind of 'misfit' between official teaching and 'home-made' teaching. I hope to venture back towards roots, ramifications and associations of education, and forward to a clarification of education's sense and meaning in today's world. Ramifications, associations, clarifications, interpretations and not deductions, proofs, theories or arguments are what this chapter is interested in.

And yet all this still sounds very cognitively controlled, very deliberate; a simple matter of knock and it shall be opened. So as I set out now, walking back and down into education's past, I remember that the word pedagogy comes from the Greek '*pedagogue*', one who walked beside the pupil accompanying him to school. But it is poetry's rhythmic 'feet' that I hope will be my pedagogue, that will help me 'measure' what I may find as I set out in this chapter. Like the hand of an older brother or sister, I reach out to the poetic as I approach the door and knock on the portal that is the word *'educare'* ...

I hear footsteps inside approaching this door. Suddenly, standing here, I feel like a Junior Infant who has just knocked on the door of that archetypal space, 'The Master's Room'. The door opens revealing an underground cave of some sort with light at the far end. It takes my eyes a moment or two to adjust to the darkness, but as they do so my hearing sharpens ... voices are talking ... gradually I distinguish shadowy pictures on the walls of the cave ... A voice begins, 'I want you to go on to picture the enlightenment or ignorance of our human condition somewhat as follows. Imagine an underground chamber like a cave, with a long entrance open to the daylight ...'.[3] The Master is in full flight.

Plato's Cave

If the view that Western philosophy is a series of footnotes to Plato[4] is reasonably accurate, then it would not be far from the truth to say that our Western philosophy of education is a series of footnotes to Plato's *Republic* and that our educational practice is a colouring-in of his simile of the cave. In this simile Plato draws a picture of education in one of the senses of the word *'educare'*, i.e. 'to lead out'. In short, the simile portrays education as a craft or *techne,* a rationally employed skill. The aim of employing such a skill is to lead those in the cave, who, for whatever reason, are looking in the wrong direction and therefore cannot see the truth, via a series of stages from the illusory to the real, from darkness to light, from ignorance to knowledge, from the base to the sublime:

'First he [the slave] would find it easier to look at shadows, next at the reflections of men and other objects in water, and later on at the objects themselves. After that he would find it easier to observe the heavenly bodies and the sky itself at night, and to look at the light of the moon and the stars rather than at the sun and its light by day.'
'Of course.'
'The thing he would be able to do last would be to look directly at the sun itself and gaze at it without using reflections in water or any other medium, but as it is in itself.'
'That must come last.'[5]

The whole simile offers an image of education as a movement out of illusion towards reality, out of ignorance into enlightenment and, critically, in a Greek culture that 'extolled the bright side of everything to the exclusion of the dark',[6] gave precedence to light, hence to sight and to the eye, and in particular the eye of the mind as the organ by which we learn. It endorses education as an attempt to lead human beings from the limitations of the physical senses, from the physical eye to the mind's eye, and to set their sights on the sun, the Greek symbol of ideal form, other-worldly source of truth, of light, of life, of the eternal Good – in short, of the bright heights to which humans should fix their gaze and seek through education to fix the gaze of others. Basically it suggested education as a guided movement out of darkness into light, a movement that is reflected in our three-tiered education system, or ten-stepped qualification system today. But it is probably best to let the Master himself interpret his own simile:

'But our argument indicates that the capacity for knowledge is innate in each man's mind, and that the organ by which he learns is like an eye which cannot be turned from darkness to light unless the whole body is turned; in the same way the mind as a whole must be turned away from the world of change until its eye can bear to look straight at reality, and at the brightest of all realities which is what we call the good. Isn't that so?'

'Yes.'

'Then this turning around of the mind itself might be made a subject of professional skill [*techne*] which would effect the conversion as easily and effectively as possible. It would not be concerned to implant sight, but to ensure that someone who had it already was not either turned in the wrong direction or looking in the wrong way.'

'That may well be so.'[7]

There is little 'may be' about it. Western philosophy and education have been hallmarked by this outstanding Athenian. Subsequent Christian theology and religious education in its initial elaborations by St Augustine and St Thomas Aquinas bear the hallmark of this Greek thought-pattern too – education as the employment of a skill, the aim being to 'effect the conversion' of the student. It is not my intention to trace the chronology of Greek philosophical influence from Augustine and Thomas Aquinas to the Enlightenment to technical rationalism, Popper and company and on to the present day. Others better qualified than I have already done so. My interest is in working poetically with images, symbols and sounds. Therefore I will direct my attention to the simile itself and to its symbols of light and darkness. I have knocked on the door and my interest now is in entering into Plato's cave imaginatively, to see but more importantly perhaps, since it is dark in there, to *hear* for myself what is going on.

My eye is drawn towards the brightness at the entrance to the cave but voices catch my ear and, not knowing at first which way to turn, I eventually give my attention to voices in a drama taking place in the shadows of the cave. I can just about make out silhouettes of a man in a battle helmet and two women, one breastfeeding a baby, the other pleading with the man in battle dress. I hear them talking urgently.

This drama is a scene from Book VI of Homer's *Iliad*. The man is Hector, the baby is his son who is being fed by his wet-nurse. The other woman is Andromache, Hector's wife. Although dressed for battle, Hector at this moment is not fighting but trying to prevent it. Hector is the ideal hero, someone who, even though he is a leader and a soldier, can be seen as tender, loving and gentle in his relations with others. In spite of – or as well as – embodying such qualities he can and does fight with total courage, dedication and commitment to his men. In this way he is a complex threshold figure in whom the capacity to do violence coexists with deep human compassion, allowing him to occupy a mental and emotional threshold between the embodiment, and the questioning, of traditional understandings of that quality Greeks held above all other qualities: *arête*,[8] nobleness of character. Symbolically this piece of drama, casting shadows like a puppet show on the wall of the cave, is located on a physical threshold – the city walls, on one side of which there is relative safety and on the other side there is considerable danger. Andromache pleads with Hector to adopt a defensive strategy by commanding his men from the walls of the city and not from the front line of battle, thereby increasing his chances of surviving to live out his life with his wife and son. Dearly though he loves her and his baby and would gladly do as she suggests, Hector's martial values and his noble character which has been 'well educated' prevent him from acceding to her request. In reply to her request he says:

All this weighs on my mind too dear woman.
But I would die of shame to face the men of Troy
and the Trojan women trailing their long robes
if I would shrink from battle now a coward.
Nor does the spirit urge me on that way.
I've learned it all too well. To stand up bravely
always to fight in the front ranks of Trojan soldiers.

In this scene we have a description of the traditional tragic
hero whose situation is rendered all the more poignant for
being cast in the midst of tender love-relations. But I wish to
look at this scene in an educational context. I deliberately
choose to interpret it as a drama involving parents,
teacher/nurturer and child. The scene above continues:

In the same breath shining Hector reached down
for his son – but the boy recoiled
cringing against his nurse's full breast
screaming at the sight of his own father,
terrified by the flashing bronze, the horsehair crest,
the great ridge of the helmet nodding, bristling terror –
so it struck his eyes. And his loving father laughed,
his mother laughed as well, and glorious Hector,
quickly lifting his helmet from his head,
set it down on the ground, fiery in the sunlight,
and raising his son he kissed him, tossed him in his
arms,
lifting a prayer to Zeus and the other deathless Gods;
Zeus, all you immortals! Grant this boy, my son
may be like me, and rule all Troy in power
and one day let them say, 'He is a better man than his
father –
when he comes home from battle wearing the bloody
gear

of the mortal enemy he has killed in war –
a joy to his mother's heart'.
    So Hector prayed and placed his son in the arms of
his loving wife.
Andromache pressed the child to her scented breast,
smiling through her tears.

Poetry and the epic was the Greek citizen's bible, so it is not all that surprising to imagine Homer's characters, like figures from an Old Greek Testament, talking to Zeus in Plato's cave. Much has been written about Homer and the great epics, the *Odyssey* and the *Iliad*. I wish to draw attention to one comment only: that of Simone Weil in relation to the *Iliad*:

> The true hero, the subject, the centre of the *Iliad* is force. Force as man's instrument, force as man's master, force before which human flesh shrinks back. The human soul in this poem is shown always in its relation to force: swept away, blinded by the force to which it is subjected. Those who had dreamed that force, thanks to progress, now belonged to the past have seen the poem as a historical document; those who can see that force, today as in the past, is the centre of all human history, find in the *Iliad* its most beautiful, its purest mirror.[9]

In Book VI of the *Iliad* the focus is on Hector upon whose shoulders the total war effort rests. Hector's true nature is as much peace-maker as fighter. In this section of the poem the image of the 'glorious Hector' may be taken to represent the Greek embodiment of 'ideal form', both as an image of light – flashing bronze, helmet fiery in the sunlight and so on – and as an ideal embodiment of *arête* – 'glorious Hector'. Here, the one who is turned, indeed forced towards the shining brightness, towards that ideal form, is the child, Hector's baby son. In this section of the epic we have a significant movement prefiguring the movement within the simile of the cave. We have in Hector's action a reflection of Plato's image of *educare*, i.e. education as a moving out towards the light:

> Then think what would naturally happen to them if ... one of them were ... suddenly compelled to stand up and turn his head and look and walk towards the fire ... and if he were made to look directly at the light of the fire, it would hurt his eyes and he would retreat back ... And if ... he were forcibly dragged up the steep and rugged ascent and not let go until he had been dragged out into the sunlight, the process would be a painful one, to which he would much object ...[10]

Like the inhabitant of the cave, this primary piece of Greek epic portrays the child, body and soul turned towards the light. But education has another root image coming from the Greek word '*educare*' or '*educere*' meaning 'to nourish' or to nurse: to 'rear young'. This definition finds its earliest and most accurate expression in the image of nursing or breastfeeding. As an image it has not been so prevalent in the history of the development of our education system. I believe it is significant that, in this passage involving the parents, the child and the original nurse-as-image-of-education, the child is turned *towards* the image of light and ideal form, the shining brightness, the epitome of Greek *arête,* the noble hero represented by Hector – one image of education – while what he is turned *away* from is the nurse and the nurturing process which is the other image of education. In such a situation the reaction of the child is critical. Like the slave in the cave, the child 'much objects'; he recoils, 'Terrified by the flashing bronze, the horsehair crest/The great ridge of the helmet nodding, bristling terror –/so it struck his eyes'. Terrified by the sight of this overwhelming brightness, the child is taken, screaming and crying from where, one might say educationally, he was 'negotiating' his needs at that moment. Mirroring the movement of the Greek soul, and in it, the 'soul' of Greek education, the child is swept away from the cradle of his nurse's arms, within which he is being nourished and *forced* out into the brightness that struck his eyes with 'bristling terror'.

The shining glorious Hector reaches, not 'out' to his son but 'down' (with its inherent hierarchical value) to the child at the breast and the child 'recoiled/cringing'. Having separated the child from the image of education embodied in the nourishing function Hector, removing his helmet before he prays, forces the child *up* towards the sun and the deathless god of gods, Zeus. He prays a blessing on his son that he may be a better man than his father. Having already acknowledged that he, Hector, has 'learned it all too well', he therefore prays that his son may learn it all even better. This prayer acts as an instrument of divine sanction, an act that consecrates the child to the education that leads in the direction of the light, the sun, towards ideal form, the epitome of a better learning, an en-lightened education. I interpret this moment in Homer's *Iliad* as a prefiguring of the orientation of education away from one archetypal image towards another, i.e. away from education as nourishment towards education as leading out towards light.

In this incident from the *Iliad* I believe we see the educational dimension of Simone Weil's interpretation. We see *the soul of Greek education*, in relation to force, in relation to the educational will to mastery of human nature, swept up and away, blinded by the light force, the sun, to which it is subjected. I interpret in this parent–child–teacher triad a key educational shift, the subordination of physical and instinctive nurturing ways of teaching/learning to another more forcefully constructed way of teaching/ learning, of mastering the subject in both senses, i.e. curriculum content and pupil/teacher. In addition, given that the *Iliad* itself embodies a critical moment of transition from oral tradition to written, it may also be interpreted as a shift from teaching as an oral tradition (based on the ear, the voice, hearing, speaking and listening – all of which are intensified in darkness) to a written tradition (the eye, the visual, the written, the 'notable'). Along with the demotion of teaching and learning as nurturing, the ramifications of this shift, educationally speaking, disadvantaged poetry and its role in and as a model of education since it too is primarily oral, aural and – at its purest – divined rather than mastered.

A shift from one image of education to another may, at first glance, seem unworthy or incapable of carrying the heavy significance I attach to it above. It would not of course be surprising that one would think so, having been brought up within an education system more technically than poetically inclined, more likely to be convinced by scientific proof than persuaded by poetic imagery. However, remembering with George Steiner:

> The totality of Homer, the capacity of the *Iliad* and *Odyssey* to serve as repertoire for most of the principal postures of Western consciousness, point to a moment of singular linguistic energy. (My own view is that the collation of the *Iliad* and the *Odyssey* coincide with the 'new immortality' of writing, with the specific transition from oral to written literature.)[11]

And remembering also what Carl Jung has in mind when he speaks about archetypal images, i.e. 'images charged with numinosity or psychic energy which becomes dynamic and from which consequences of some kind must flow',[12] the images of education as 'nourishing' or as 'leading out' are not just images, but are I believe *archetypal images* with powerful numinous energy and deep poetic roots and ramifications. In this case, the numinosity or psychic energy of these images stems at least in part from the dynamism of Homer's epic poetic voice, its mastery and its 'mustery', its summoning, of the rhythms, resonances and resources of oral tradition towards a forward drive. It is as though something in Homer's poetic voice dislodged or shifted or levered a dynamic power that began to move and effect 'Greek consequences' that continue to flow forcefully through education and its will to mastery, today. This moment within the *Iliad* may be a moment when, within the repertoire of principal postures in western educational consciousness (whether religious or general), the balance between education as an oral tradition (i.e. having to do with the mouth and ear) and as a written tradition (having to do with the eye and the visual) changed gear, or to put it musically, changed key.

This change of key may be difficult to hear given our visual-image-based culture but I describe it for myself by comparing it to a similar shift that happens courtesy of the piper Liam O'Flynn. In an instant of singular musical energy, he shifts the tune of the 'Wraggle Taggle Gypsies' into the tune of 'Tabhair Dom Do Lamh' (to be found on *Planxty Live*, 2004). It is a seemingly effortless yet seismic musical shift achieved in an instant, during which a 'keynote' from the first tune is for a split second held open, seducing the first note from the new tune to enter and pivot the old tune in a new direction. A change has taken place and, once heard, cannot be forgotten. But however programmed the shift seems in retrospect, it was first heard via the audial imagination, resonating deep down in the aural memory of the musical tradition of which tunes, pipes and piper are a part. It first vibrates in an instant of musical spontaneity between the ear of the piper and the deeper subconscious rhythms and resonances of the larger musical tradition, issuing magically, druidically into the present via drones, chanters and windpipes in the instrument itself. For Plato as for all Greeks, Homer was 'The Poet *as* Piper; he was the Authority'. He called the tune. In the Greek experience the 'unequaled Fire and Rapture which is so forcible in *Homer*' meant that 'no Man of a true poetical spirit is Master of himself while he experiences the *Iliad*'. Homer's poetry is a performance, a musical event in which 'Homer's energy, the loft and carry of his imagination … sweeps along the listener together with the performer'.[13] In the context of a shift from oral to written tradition Homer, as it were, calls Plato's educational tune and it is a tune in whose crescendo the soul of Greek educational philosophy is swept up and aloft like Hector's son, towards the light, the eye and the written. In that sweep philosophy, and with it education, is caught up and distanced from the darkness that nourishes the poetic. Plato, himself both philosopher and poet, was famously suspicious of poetry and the power of poets in education. However, *what* Plato says in this regard – for example, 'It is not that they are bad poetry or are not popular, indeed the better they are as poetry the more unsuitable they are for the ears of our children' – is only one half of the story; *how* he says this is the other half: 'I say it with hesitation, because of Homer's authority.'[14] He himself, I suspect, was caught up in the very power of which he was suspicious so that mastery of himself would never be fully complete in Plato because his eye, despite its desire for philosophical clarity of vision, would (thankfully) never be entirely free of the influence of his poetic ear. Into one of Plato's ears, Homer's epic voice hammered on, full throttle, rattle and hum. And although I can't make it out for sure, my own ear tells me it may be the perfect pitch and lyrical voice of the Greek poetess Sappho, whom Plato called 'the tenth Muse', who whispers a different kind of tune to a different beat, in Plato's other ear.[15]

The images I used at the beginning of this chapter to express my experience of teaching – always playing my teaching game on an away pitch and so on – go to the heart of a struggle within this ancient Greek ancestor Plato; it is the struggle between Plato the philosopher and Plato the poet; between his eye for clarity and his ear for mystery. Greek philosophy classified poetry as a craft or *techne*. The aim of all poetry was to make those who heard or read it feel certain things, for example to be inspired to fight more bravely or live more justly. The poet, it was supposed, would decide how he wanted his audience to feel and from that he would plan the best way of achieving that aim, through, for example, the type of poem, the kind of theme and the choice of certain words in certain order. Having worked it all out in his head thus, he would then simply execute the whole thing in writing. Surprisingly for such a controlled view of poetry, the poet in Plato knew by ear that poetry was also a gift – 'a madness' – and his suspicion of poetry arose out of his recognition that as such it was not or would never be fully under conscious control. To some extent poetry would always be just beyond conscious control; that was its power.

I suspect that a related dilemma is at the heart of how teaching is classified. To what extent is teaching a craft? All teaching aims at the learning of certain things; once you decide, or it has been decided for you, what it is you want to teach you simply work out the best way of doing it, select the appropriate means and methodologies and execute the lesson. But teachers, like poets, know that if teaching is a craft it is also a gift. Its gifted nature is directly related to poesy: its way of seeing, hearing and engaging through language with the deeper human registers in life; its recognition that some things in life, including lessons one might want others to learn, will always be to some extent beyond control. At the heart of how education talks about itself therefore is a linguistic power struggle that results in the kind of practice described by Madeleine Grumet in her book *Bitter Milk*:

> Docile, self-effacing, we hand in our lesson plans, replete with objectives and echoes of the current rationale, and then, safe behind the doors of our self-enclosed classrooms, subvert those schemes, secure in their atheoretical wisdom, intuitive rather than logical, responsive rather than initiating, nameless yet pervasive. The programmes stay on paper, the administrators' theory barred from practice, the teachers' practice barred from theory ...[16]

Behind Grumet's scenario, behind the difficulty I as a teacher faced in trying to articulate what exactly teaching is, why I could not completely buy into teaching-as-craft, as a technical–rational process, is the kind of edu-cultural silence that George Steiner reminds us of when he says that 'where power relations determine the conditions of meeting ... the patronised and the oppressed have endured behind their silences'[17] or, in the case of teachers, behind their closed classroom doors. It may be that the difficulty in articulating the vague hunch that something in my experience of teaching 'misfitted' is like the experience expressed in Darragh's (4th class) poem:

> One day
> I made myself a poem
> I tried it on
> I looked in the mirra

the buttons were done up
wrong.

Perhaps this experience is particular to me alone, but I have
a hunch that it is not. I feel that the scenario of the teacher's
practice barred from theory and the theoretician's version of
teaching barred from practice is common to many. If so, to
an extent teaching today is a matter of enduring behind the
silence, behind the classroom door. Beyond the classroom
door the latest educational theory takes to the stage. But too
often, the latest educational theories are ancient Greek
leanings in Modern disguise. The real challenge in teaching
today I believe is to counter-balance those philosophical
leanings by searching, groping or listening for a language
like that of Darragh's poem, a language that can express the
nature of teaching as other than technical craft – teaching as
gift, a language that has the ear of the poet as well as the eye
of the philosopher.

Education as Nurturing

So far, my explorations lead me to believe that a
fundamental shift in emphasis and power-relations took
place between two archetypal images of education. This
shift orientated education's understanding and therefore its
way of talking about itself away from an intuitive nurturing
towards a rational leading out. Education imitated art. Now
I wish to return to the image of education as
nursing/nurturing to see what it may restore to education
and to educational language. The baby at the full breast is
an original image of *educare* and it is to this image that I
turn my attention. In doing so I want to explore the
significance of the image as a model of an educational
process that sees the *teacher as a nourisher* regardless of
whether the teacher is male or female. It is not gender,
biology or how babies are fed that is at issue here. Rather it

is whether or not and to what extent primary education is essentially a pedagogic process of nurturing by an experienced, responsive intuition that has sunk a shaft deep into the tradition of which it is a part, over and against a purely rational leading out towards knowledge, mastery etc. Hector does not return the child to its nurse but to its mother. Once the child is handed over to the mother the nurse is no longer relevant and is not mentioned again in the passage. She is disempowered and dispensed with, implying the dispensing with education as nurturing.

Before dispensing with this educational image it is worth exploring what it has to offer education by way of an alternative understanding of itself. Traditionally, the child has been thought of as passive in the feeding process, but there is evidence that the baby plays an active role in negotiating the meeting of its need for nourishment:

> ... when it is allowed to happen, the relationship between a baby and the breast is quite different from that with a bottle because it is quite dynamic. A baby is actively involved in the milk manufacture, because it is the baby's suckling which keeps the whole process going. This is why the English word 'suckle' is so appropriate; it means the action of both the mother and the baby who are co-workers.[18]

Breastfeeding therefore, as an image, can model education as a dynamic process, a process in which the pupil is not the passive recipient of a curricular product supplied by a teacher – male or female – and behind them a department of education, but an active negotiator with the teacher in the meeting of the primary educational need: to be nourished in living the life of a child/teacher to the full, now and for the future. It is in the process of meeting these aims that pupil and teacher constitute each other as pupil and teacher in the same way that mother or father and baby constitute each other as parent and child. My children have a critical influence in making me the parent I am; my pupils have a similar influence in making me the teacher I am. As an image it embodies an understanding of teaching and learning as interdependent functions, as a mutual engagement in which process and product are held in healthy tension, allowing joint ownership of both by the agencies of teacher and pupil alike. It is an image in which mastery and control of a process (or pupil or teacher) via programmes, rationale, aims, objectives, methodologies and so on yield critical access to education as interdependency *within* a process.

The modern decline in the practice of breastfeeding today and its replacement with formula or bottle-feeding allows the possibility of developing the image and interpreting the bottle educationally as 'ideal form', as controlled process, and applying this metaphor to education. There are many anxieties surrounding the birth of a baby, especially a first, since it provides the original teaching/learning opportunity from which subsequent lessons are learned. Indeed one might say that the primary educational act at the very basis of life itself is the shared instinct of mother and child for 'feeding'. It is the original site of interdependent teaching and learning. Much anxiety often surrounds the feeding process – fear of not being able to understand, of misinterpreting the baby's non-verbal language, i.e. the non-speech language of cries, the additional fear that this lack of understanding or misinterpretation might prevent a vulnerable human being's basic needs being adequately met, thereby creating the painful experiences of a hungry baby and an 'inadequate' mother. These anxieties might be thought of as the mother's but there is no reason why the baby might not also feel these anxieties at an instinctive level. At the heart of the mother/baby relationship therefore lies a deep human vulnerability and inadequacy in the face of another's needs, an anxiety that ultimately translates into a question about the adequacy or inadequacy of language, especially non-verbal language, to relate; language *as* human relation.

When it comes to negotiating this anxiety, if one bottle-feeds, one can look at the bottle and quantify in terms of fluid milligrams how much the baby has taken; it is then easier to establish whether the language being 'cried out' is communicating hunger or has some other meaning. Empirical evidence therefore comes to play a significant role in the interpretive process and consequently in the emotional process of relieving anxiety by offering greater certainty in the form of 'bottled proof'. But in terms of breastfeeding, layers of anxiety, confusion and doubt based on fear of misinterpretation may build upon one another and even spiral out of control, with painful consequences for both the processes' participants, since the empirical evidence of how much food one's baby is getting is absent from the situation. Compared to the bottle's contents, which may be analysed, measured, quantified, certified and delivered effectively, breastfeeding images an educational process that is, to say the least, ambiguous, resistant to empirical measurement and scientific accountability.

With the move away from the education as nursing and its replacement with a 'leading out towards the light', education becomes the technically enlightened, scientific 'way of the bottle'. In the matter of education's content its curriculum becomes a kind of formula food and in terms of teacher and methodology a kind of formula feeding, a way of delivering educational content with greater certainty, efficiency and accountability. By comparison, the image of breastfeeding pictures an educational content less amenable to analysis, and much of its nurturing 'methodology' arises out of the non- or pre-verbal experienced intuitive that is also striving towards speech and intimately bound up with interpretation. Its assessment procedures tacitly and intuitively gauge the development of the child/pupil (and mother/teacher). Its assessment is based on the wisdom of past experience, which is difficult to articulate in the objective, deductive, quantifying discourse of education today, a discourse described by Michael Apple as one that is '... increasingly framed in economic terms – in the language of production, rationalisation and standardisation – the machinery of the mechanisation of education'.[19] In short it is difficult to articulate education in technical, mechanical terms when it is not conducted solely as a technical–mechanical process. Breastfeeding does not offer measurable empirical evidence in the same way that bottle-feeding does and therefore cannot keep anxiety at bay. It requires that anxiety be negotiated, taken on trust, a trust based on the wisdom of experience with sufficient faith to believe in what is orally and traditionally 'being passed on'. As an educational image or an educational model, therefore, it may be said that formula food and formula feeding provide an image of the preferred option in education today. It is these mechanised ways of nourishing/teaching/learning that are seen to have the measure of education.

Returning to the scene from the *Iliad* as a poetic act in which education's focus on the physical body, its food and its feeding, is sidelined in favour of leading out of the mind towards the light, this piece of poetry prefigures Plato's philosophical concern that education, as represented by his simile of the cave, rises above the body's basic physicality towards a higher order; its concern with the eye of the mind rather than the physical eye. Its concern for higher order things of the mind, not along with physical concerns, but over and above them, mirrors a trend in education to relegate the physical to a place of lesser importance than the education of the intellect. It is also mirrored in the theological scenting of religious education to follow a course leading towards things of the mind/spirit and away from the physical. In doing so another key modeller of education as nourishing, Jesus of Nazareth, the body become bread, broken, blessed and shared, becomes as redundant as our Greek nurse. In this sense general education and religious education have both been significantly 'scented' to lead in the direction of the light over and above the physical order, of not just the physical human body but the planetary body too. The moment of psychic effect created in this epic, when education is taken from the nurse and forced out in the direction of Greek brightness, has influenced not just general but religious education.

So far I have explored a shift in educational images and emphasis, and I have identified that shift as a downgrading or demotion of education as an instinctive but experienced nurturing process in favour of a more scientifically or consciously controlled methodological process: a bottle-feeding. As I make ready to leave the cave, however, the unnamed, silenced and about to be dismissed nurse points, as though suggesting to me that there is something I have missed.

At the heart of the breastfeeding process is a question of language, communication and interpretation: in short the grammar of interdependent 'being'.[20] How do two human beings reach out to try to understand and contain each other when the usual means of such communication – words – are meaningless? According to this image communication is conducted via two physical human attributes – milk and tears (cries). These attributes are identified by the philosopher Julia Kristeva as 'metaphors of non-speech, of a semiotics that linguistic communication does not account for';[21] in other words, at the heart of this powerful image lies the weakness of language, the powerlessness of words to conduct communication in this primary area of human experience. In a sense this situation mirrors the dilemma at the beginning of this chapter: how to communicate about teaching when I do not have words to say what I mean and the person I want to communicate with has words which are meaningless to me? If I and the other with whom I try to communicate look to this image of education then we will come to know that at the heart of education as nurturing lies the weakness of language, the powerlessness of words to account for the deepest areas of human learning because these very areas often conduct themselves beyond words; in silence or, in an educational sense perhaps, behind those closed doors in tears that may sometimes be the pupil's and sometimes the teacher's. The image of the nurturing process offers the possibility of an education that educates in the face of the weakness of language containing the fundamental anxiety around it, sufficiently, rather than taking flight from it via dubious technical mastery and control over language. As a teacher, and thanks to poetry, I do not find it difficult to accept that somewhere deep down in the teaching/learning relationship is a communication beyond words. However, a modern education that has built its reputation on methodological assess-ability, measure-ability, diagnos-ability and correct-ability would find the idea that some area of teaching and learning lay beyond 'accountability', quite unacceptable. In dealing with – or, perhaps more accurately, in denying – this vulnerability, by speaking of education in a language that tries to define it beyond interpretation, to tie every single 'strand' of experience down with those Lilliputian threads, by taking flight from human vulnerability in language, those ancient Greek ancestors who took the same flight have landed in modern education's backyard.

In terms of the role of poetry and the poetic in education, being the exemplar that it is of language at work on life and life at work on language and inviting as it does layer upon layer of interpretation, poetry carries the societal anxiety about language into the heart of the classroom. Poetry's role in educational process as the 'deepest education there is' is at odds with the ancient Greek and modern-day technicist drive to escape interpretation's ambiguity by taking refuge in scientific language that seeks to dispense with interpretation altogether. However, it is in deep sympathy with the image of nurturing; after all, 'Our poesy is as a gum which oozes/from whence 'tis nourished'.[22] Inevitably under the force of will to mastery in education today, curriculum is managed by being desiccated into strands, units, themes, aims, objectives, methodologies, and so on. Conversely, poetry writing as a model of education revels in working precisely and intimately with language and therefore with life. Language and life are like the teacher and the pupil, mutually and interdependently engaged within a process that when it is poetic is at its most creative, its most educational, its most life-giving and still always aware of its limitations, but revelling in them nonetheless. Tara's poem about losing her first tooth (Chapter 5) offers a succinct metaphor for the nature of the relationship between language and life, and indeed between teaching and learning, between poetry and education. It images the obsession they have with each other:

> A shaky tooth
> and a pushy tongue
> just can't leave
> each other alone.

If the shift in archetypal image and emphasis in education that I have outlined here is valid then it is likely that the counterbalance of this shift will be found not in, for example, 'growing' the kind of discourse contained in the present volume of Primary Curriculum from two texts (1971) to twenty-two texts (1999) to however many more in the future. It is more likely to be found by fostering a more poetic educational discourse that can talk about education more fully, more humanely; one that can give education a home ground on which to play.

The difficulty today for teachers of articulating what it is that truly 'makes me a teacher', indeed of saying what genuine education is or can be, is the difficulty of generating this different, counterbalancing kind of educational discourse. Another dimension of the difficulty is that this discourse will be generated within an already existing set of educational power relations. Teachers have to try to speak in technical terminology about something which we do not practice solely as a *techne*; something that is more than a scientific reasoning, something that is 'other-wise'. We struggle to speak our wisdom and experience, to tell what we know, but are caught in a gap between the kind of knowledge we are *supposed* to possess and the minute-to-minute knowing that our teaching actually embodies. We are haunted in a sense by 'a knowing' that we cannot name and plagued by a meticulously named 'knowing' that is not enough. We struggle with a silence in which the language in which we might begin to speak our experience – poetic language, the language of images – is not a recognised 'educational discourse'. Despite the considerable difficulty, therefore, we too, like Wordsworth, must try to 'give while yet we may/a substance and a life to what we feel' about teaching.

It is out of the struggle between silence and educational terminology that a poetic way of talking about how we teach and learn, and the nature of our experience as we do so, must be fostered. To foster the language in which this kind of educational conversation can be held requires imagination, because imagination is an indispensable agent in the creation of the meaning of what it is to be a teacher. That meaning can only be created in and through language. This requires faith in the poetic as a way of tuning in to those inner reaches, those moments in our teaching lives when intuitions tell us without words that something has been really good, or tells us that something is not quite as it should be or that, however it is, something feels like it should be otherwise. Heaney has said of the poet: '... in practice, you proceed by your own experience of what it is to write what you consider to be a successful poem. You survive in your own esteem not by corroboration of theory but by the trust in certain moments of satisfaction which you know intuitively to be moments of extension.'[23] The same holds true for the practice of teaching; you survive, not by the corroboration of theory but by trust in certain moments in your teaching when you just know, 'That was good'. To imagine is to give credit (creed-ence) to intuitions – of the good and the mistaken. To imagine is to muster whatever linguistic and pre-linguistic resources one can towards articulation. To imagine is to act by giving expression to whatever is trying to 'get said'. By uncovering deeper, more complex dimensions to what it means to be a teacher, possibilities for new ways of acting and being in the world of education are realised. The reality of what it is to be a teacher is deepened, *authorised* by experience. Resistance to notes and methodologies and technical educational discourse may be my particular experience, my particular prejudice, and it may not be applicable to other teachers but, suspended between the extremes of educational rationalism and the weakness of language at the core of human existence, only an education intimate with the poetic can speak the complex reality that is teaching and learning.

Conclusion

Entering through the portal that is the word '*educare*' I have sought to trace my steps back to discover the voices of my educational ancestors speaking in education today. I have tried to do so by entering Plato's cave, not intellectually but by feeling my own way into it, by groping around in its darkness, listening to the strangeness of the Greek voices whispering therein, peering at the flickering shadows on the walls and wondering in writing what all this might mean. The flickering shadows on the walls reminded me of Louis le Brocquy's series of ink-images on the Táin. Commenting on those images the artist says that:

> Graphic images, if any, should grow spontaneously and even physically from the matter on the printed text ... It is as shadows thrown by the text that they are there.[24]

It is as shadows thrown by the fire that burned in Plato's cave (doubtless a projection of the fire that burned in Plato the philosopher, poet and teacher too) that I offer in this chapter *my* extension of his text. It is not the images themselves or the particular characters that are important – you might go in his cave and see and hear other visual or aural images. But what is important is that, to go in there imaginatively, with poetry as your guide, is to come out understanding education differently. For that much I can and do thank Plato.

In this chapter I have suggested that Plato, picking up the will-to-force in the rhythms and resonances and imagery of the Greek soul, masterfully presented to the Greek eye and ear in Homeric epic, was swept along in this powerful current, bringing education with him. The paradox for Plato in this situation was that he himself fell victim to what he was suspicious of – the power of poetry in education – and yet it seems to me that that very power offers Plato and today's Greek-sponsored education their main hope of rescue or redress. Between them, Homer and Plato orientated Greek education away from a process of mutual interdependency between teacher and pupil within a context imaged in the nurse and the process of breastfeeding and re-orientated it towards education as a *techne*, a pre-programmed process 'leading out of darkness towards light'. There is no doubt that both these images have authenticity; my quarrel is not with education leading from darkness to light by means of reasoned steps. My problem is with these images' predominance. Therefore the effort in this work has been, as Simone Weil said, 'to add weight to the lighter scale'. After all, at least half of one's games should be played at home!

These are my thoughts as I exit Plato's cave. But as I make my way out of the cave, the Master's voice still ringing in my ear, I have a strange encounter. The silent, unnamed nurse/teacher, steps forward momentarily from the shadows. She looks me in the eye and I look at her. Though she still does not speak, her silence is profound. I note it. In the instant of that visual exchange nothing is said but much is meant. It is as if she wants to let me know that although her voice is not being heard, she continues to be a presence, she will not be 'written' off. Then just as spontaneously as she stepped forward, she steps back into the shadows and I exit the cave, where my poet-guide is already waiting to escort me into the next chapter.

Notes

1. *Preoccupations: Selected Prose 1968–1978*, London, Faber and Faber, 1980, p. 52.
2. For an in-depth study see *Back To The Rough Ground*, op. cit.
3. Plato, *The Republic*, London, Penguin Classics, 1974, p. 256.

4. For more on the subject see Padraig Hogan's *Custody and Courtship of Experience: Western Education in Philosophical Perspective*, Dublin, The Columba Press, 1995.

5. *The Republic*, p. 258.

6. Hederman, M.P., *Kissing The Dark: Connecting with the Unconscious*, Dublin, Veritas, 1999, p. 27.

7. *The Republic*, pp. 258–9.

8. *Arête* may be described as 'that peculiar excellence that makes a thing or horse or soldier or hero, the best, most effective of their kind ... and ideal of human worth in the character that unites nobility of action with nobility of mind'. Knox, intro to *The Iliad*, Penguin Classics, 1991.

9. Ibid., p. 29.

10. *The Republic*, pp. 257–8.

11. *After Babel: Aspects of Language and Translation*, Oxford University Press, 1975, p. 23.

12. *Man and his Symbols*, London, Picador, 1964, p. 87.

13. Lee, D., Translator's Preface to *The Iliad*, London, Penguin Classics, 1991.

14. *The Republic*, Part Three, Education: The First Stage, pp. 70–88.

15. 'After his nephew had sung one of Sappho's songs over the wine, Solon of Athens, the son of Execestides, told the lad to teach it to him immediately. When someone asked why he was so eager, Solon replied, 'So that I may die knowing it'. Sappho was considered one of Greece's finest poets. Her voice was very different to Homer's – a treble rather than a bass.

    Solon's instantaneous and uncomplicated delight in Sappho's poetry typifies the attitude of the Ancient Greeks to her work. She was considered one of their finest poets, an integral part of their cultural history. Her face was engraved on coinage, her statue erected, her portrait painted on vases. Many ancient commentators praised her literary genius, while Plato, among others, called her 'the tenth Muse'. For more on Sappho's poetry see *Sappho: Poems and Fragments*, Trans. Josephine Balmer, Brilliance Books, Plain Edition, 1984.

16. *Bitter Milk: Women and Teaching*, Amherst, The University of Massachusetts Press, 1988, p. 25.

17. Steiner also says that 'In most societies and throughout history the status of women has been akin to that of children. Both groups are maintained in a condition of privileged inferiority.

Both suffer obvious modes of exploitation – sexual, legal,
economic – while benefiting from a mythology of special regard.
Under sociological and psychological pressure, both minorities
have developed internal codes of communication and defence.
There is a language world of women as there is of children.'
(*After Babel*, p. 38.)

Given that classrooms are increasingly spaces inhabited by
women and children, the language world of the classroom is, I
believe, a language world of internal codes of communication
and defence.

18. Palmer, G, *The Politics of Breastfeeding*, London, Pandora,
    1998, p. 19.
19. *Teachers and Texts*, London, Routledge and Keegan Paul, 1986,
    p. 27.
20. 'Eros and language mesh at every point. Intercourse and
    discourse, copula and copulation are sub-classes of the dominant
    fact of communication. They arise from the life need of the ego
    to reach out and comprehend in the two vital senses of
    "understanding" and "containment" another human being.

    The seminal and semantic functions (is there ultimately an
    etymological link?) determine the genetic and social structure of
    human experience. Together they construe the grammar of
    being.' *After Babel*, p. 39.
21. From *The Kristera Reader* (ed. Toril Moi) Basil/Blackness, 1986,
    p. 174.
22. *Preoccupations*, p. 33. (The quote is from Shakespeare: *Timon
    of Athens.*)
23. *Preoccupations*, p. 54.
24. *The Táin*, Trans. Thomas Kinsella, Dublin, Oxford University
    Press in association with The Dolmen Press, 1969; Intro. Artist's
    Note.

2 Into Darkness

My explorations in the preceding chapter lead me to suspect that a consequence of the orientation of education towards the light has been to accentuate one strain and one way of talking about education and to silence another. It has accentuated a technical–rational voice and silenced what I suspect is a more poetic voice. Therefore, within the teaching tradition that I have inherited there are those who have strong voices and abundant speech, for whom education's language is logical, a resource to which they seem to have unlimited access.[1] For others it is not so. To use the language of educational scientism may technically and, at times, usefully analyse a child's performance, a programme's contents or a teacher's assessment of things, but it can hardly begin to describe the actual child or the pedagogic subtext that is the live, moment-to-moment relationship between pupil(s) and teacher or the conversation of the teacher with herself. For others, as I said at the beginning of this book, the language that education speaks today is not our first language; it is not our educational 'mother tongue'; it is not the primary language in which we make educational sense and meaning. It leaves many of us classroom practitioners at a disadvantage when it comes to speaking deeply and passionately about who we are and what we do. It deports our conversations about what we do to places and occasions when we gather socially and informally and usually *outside* the school. And if this is not our spoken language, neither is it our written language. We do not express ourselves as teachers in it; what we put on paper is written con*firm*ation of our con*form*ation to official policies, prescriptions and perceptions of what we ought to be doing. In the power relations of education we reassure those in authority that we are compliant, no threat. It is to the lighter scale in the power relations between these voices that I think Homer's nurse adds the weight of her silence and therefore I feel a strange connection to her. It is as though today our teacher voice and our teacher silence are shared with her; if we find a voice with which to speak formally, authentically and authoritatively about teaching and learning, it will be hers, restored. She symbolises for me the continuing presence of the teacher who endures behind their lost voice. As I emerge from Plato's cave out into the light of a new chapter, I look around me, preoccupied with my thoughts about light and darkness and language in education. I wonder as I emerge if there is any way to counterbalance or redress the situation. What would be needed? An image, an energy or an archetype closer to home than that version of the Greek image which has predominated, perhaps, or some presence or authority that might be of sufficient stature to exercise a counterbalancing effect, that could stand up to it all. But where might I find such an authority, such a presence? At least in the preceding chapter I knew I was in search of Plato and I knew to knock on the door of the word *educare*. But where do I go from here?

Musing on this dilemma, I reach and take hold of the outstretched hand of my poet-guide again. She escorts me to a place in the Irish educational landscape where a young child is watching a man digging, shovelling, slashing briars … the man appears to be clearing out an overgrown drain between two fields. Curious, I approach.

Undine
He slashed briars, shovelled up grey silt
To give me right of way in my own drains.
And I ran quick for him, cleaned out my rust.

He halted, saw me finally disrobed,
Running clear, with apparent unconcern.
Then he walked by me. I rippled and I churned

Where ditches intersected near the river
Until he dug a spade deep in my flank
And took me to him. I swallowed his trench

Gratefully, dispersing myself for love
Down in his roots, climbing his brassy grain –
But once he knew my welcome, I alone

Could give him subtle increase and reflection.
He explored me so completely, each limb
Lost its cold freedom. Human warmed to him.[2]

I believe this poem offers itself as a metaphor for the educational dilemma I have been trying to articulate. It is a metaphor for what has happened to Irish education. Seamus Heaney describes the origins of this poem as:

an orphaned memory, without a context, obviously a very early one, of watching a man clearing out an old spongy growth from a drain between two fields, focusing in particular on the way the water began to run free and rinse itself clean of the soluble mud and make its own little channels and currents. And this image was gathered into a more conscious reading of the myth being about the liberating humanising effect of sexual encounter. Undine was a cold girl who got what the dictionary called a soul, through the experience of physical love.[3]

The word 'water' is related to the words *'vater'* and *'vates'*, the Roman title for a poet or diviner. The Undine, this 'cold girl' or this 'girl out in the cold', may therefore be interpreted as a poetic-spirit. In early Irish literature poetic skill is often described as 'fair stream' (*find-shruth*) and flowing waters – especially those of the Boyne – were deemed to contain poetic inspiration. Therefore this *'vates-spiritus'* may have origins in a Celtic feminine. The poetry of pre-Christian Ireland, just like the poetry of ancient Greece had considerable influence socially and in education.[4] It is possible, therefore, to read the poem as a myth about edu-culture,[5] about the benefits in terms of 'soul' for both education and poetry when the two have intercourse. It offers an image of the inter-taming of poetry and life, language and learning. It offers an image of an ancient poetic spirit no longer confident of right of way in its own drains, a stifled stream unable to inspire education by irrigating its channels as it had once done. The poem presents a metaphor for how poetry's way with words and images, its rhythms and resonances, its eye and ear for reality's deeper registers, the free-flow of its influence in and out of the drains and ditches of the educational landscape had become clogged, its imaginative ripplings and churnings repressed. This staunching caused education to stagnate in a kind of sump-hole over which, in an educational sense, 'spongy growth' spread rapidly. Exposure to light is one means of such rapid growth promotion. In orientating education towards light, the influential Greek philosophic germinated educational seeds that sprouted and spread due to the eventual winning out of light over darkness in mythology and in the archetypal imagery of education. When Christianity, inlaid as it was with Greek thought patterns, took root in Ireland through the monastic and diocesan school systems, those seeds grew rapidly. With the decline of the lay bardic schools whose educational processes emphasised the dark and the poetic, any hope of counterbalancing the effects of over-exposure disappeared and consequently education 'bolted'.

I do not make it my business here to delve into the chronological history of the phototropic overgrowth in education from Greek philosophy to the present; my interest is in working imaginatively more so than chronologically. My effort must be to try to imitate the critical action of the digger/poet. I hope I can slash and dig so that poetic influence may be restored and stream through education again. In the words of the poem, my effort with regard to Undine is to 'explore it completely' with a view to restoring a poetic flow through an education system whose curriculum and processes continue, I believe, to be at risk of enlightenment-induced overgrowth. The task in this chapter then is to shovel up educational 'grey silt' in order to give poetry right of way; to ripple and churn in today's education system. Through the encounter of the dark, imaginative, Celtic feminine and the bright, rational, Greek masculine, the Undine of education may experience liberation and humanisation, education may experience the 'subtle increase and reflection' that the poetic alone can give. Yet, to flood the Irish educational landscape with romantic–poetic ripplings and churnings of Celticism may be no more than indulging nostalgia. Picking up Undine's standoffish vibes and 'apparent unconcern' it is important to resist a pull to be carried away, to run too quickly, to be too conveniently disrobed of the mud and silt of education's history and poetry's role within it. Too romantic an inclination to rush and gush and to surface a dark Celtic feminine in place of Greek enlightenment must be checked; it must be – in a classicist sense – disciplined. Interpretation of the poem will benefit from walking by it once again so that any eventual 'subtle increase and reflection' in education will be genuinely fruitful.

In taking a second look at this poem as a metaphor for the state of education, it is worth remembering the poet's own advice: 'The paraphraseable extensions of a poem can be as protean as possible as long as its elements remain firm.'[6] Nothing stands firmer – more sound – in a poem over time than its aural dimension. This second look then turns not to the eye to explore the poem's elements, but to the ear and the oral; it turns not to the arrangement of words on the page but, in a more musical sense, to their arrangement in the ear, to an aural process and an aural imagination that 'set[s] the darkness echoing'[7] rather than a visual one requiring light by which to see and proceed. Returning once again to Heaney's comments on this poem, he explains how:

> It was the dark pool of the sound of the word that first took me: if our auditory imaginations were sufficiently attuned to plumb and sound a vowel, to unite the most primitive and civilised associations, the word 'undine' would suffice as a poem in itself.[8]

'Undine' is a pool of sound, the depths of whose darkness is 'set echoing' by the rhythmic ebb and flow, the seduction and response of broad and slender vowel soundings. It ripples and reverberates to the broad vowelled sounds of the digger's slashing, shovelling, halting; of his spade, dug deep in the flank; and in the quick, clean, clear, slender vowel sounds rippling through the undine's newly exposed limbs. The most critical reverberation, however, comes with the moment of unification of the poem's two energies as they physically experience one another and resound climactically in the verb 'swallowed'. At this moment one's auditory imagination sinks suddenly to the depths of an obsolete meaning of that word, 'a deep hole or opening in the earth; an opening or cavity ... through which a stream disappears underground'. Having knocked and entered Plato's underground cave in the previous chapter, it is via the sound of the word 'swallow' that I now disappear down into the opening or cavity in the middle of this poem's 'swallow'. I am sucked into the swirl-pull of syllable and rhythm in the words of the poem, sinking deeper and deeper into the dark pool of sound in the word 'Undine'. All the while as I metaphorically plummet, I find my 'auditory imagination' plumbing what T.S. Eliot called:

> the feeling of syllable and rhythm [which] penetrate far below the conscious levels of thought and feeling ... sinking to *the most primitive and forgotten*, returning to an origin and bringing something back ... fusing the most ancient and civilised mentalities.[9] (my italics)

It is as though I myself am swallowed down, descending far below conscious levels of thought and feeling, returning to an origin – the original moment – in which the most primitive has been forgotten. I am in the midst of a moment from the beginning of what is claimed by some to be the oldest vernacular epic in Western literature, the *Táin Bó Cuailnge*.[10] I have journeyed in an instant from an instance of one contemporary poet's orphaned memory to an instance of the ancient poets' memory orphaned. This is how Thomas Kinsella describes the origin into which I have arrived:

How the Táin Bó Cuailnge was Found Again

The poets of Ireland one day were gathered around Senchán Torpéist, to see if they could recall the 'Táin

Bó Cuailnge' in its entirety. But they all said they knew only parts of it. Senchán asked which of his pupils in return for his blessing would travel to the land of Letha to learn the version of the Táin that a certain sage took eastward with him in exchange for the book Cuilmenn. Emaine, Ninene's grandson, set out for the east with Senchán's son Muirgen. It happened that the grave of Fergus mac Róich was on their way. They came upon the gravestone at Enloch in Connacht. Muirgen sat down at Fergus' gravestone and the others left him for a while and went looking for a house for the night.

Muirgen chanted a poem to the gravestone as though it were Fergus himself. He said to it:

> If this your royal rock/were your own self mac Róich/halted here with sages/searching for a roof/ Cuailnge we'd recover/plain and perfect Fergus.

A great mist suddenly formed around him – for the space of three days and nights he could not be found. And the figure of Fergus approached him in fierce majesty, with a head of brown hair, in a green cloak and a red embroidered tunic, with gold-hilted sword and bronze blunt sandals. Fergus recited the whole Táin, how everything had happened from start to finish. Then they went back to Senchán with their story and he rejoiced over it.[11]

Senchán's gathering of poets represents an oral culture in a moment of transitional crisis. Oracy thrived on the remembering and narration of storied lists, litanies and genealogies. One of the main responsibilities of the poet was to satirise and praise, a key component of which was knowledge of the genealogies of one's subjects. Another key function of the poet was in relation to a branch of knowledge called *dínseanchas*, or topology – lore of places and place-names. A good poet would always be able to relate as and when required how a place had got its name. If such lore was no longer remembered, then both the poet and society were in danger of completely forgetting who they were, of having no identity. The poet was therefore a keeper of memory, a recounter – not of one unified whole story or Grand Narrative, but of versions of a 'whole story'. Identity was not just a question of human parentage – from *whom* had one come – but also of place-parentage – from *where* had one come. The poet was the one charged with expressing and remembering identity on behalf of its people. Since the *Táin*, the 'biggest myth', the parent-story, with its extensive tracts of topology, and the genealogy of key characters, only existed in fragmented form, then the identity of that society was also fragmented and at risk. We have in this moment of forgottenness an ancient yet truly post-modern crisis, a moment in which a parent-story and with it, identity, are at risk of being lost.

But the question of identity is more complex still. Like much else in the Celtic world, identity was a three-fold rather than a two-fold phenomenon. As well as human parentage and place-parentage, the following extract suggests that *word*-parentage played a part in the story of identity and its crises.

> ... versions agree in stating that the Táin was an ancient tale the manuscript of which had been given in exchange for the 'Culmen', or 'Summit [of learning]'. This Culmen ... has been identified by T. Ó'Máille with the famous 'Etymologiae' written in the early seventh century by Isodore of Seville ...[12]

In the exchange of the *Táin* for the *Etymologiae* there is an inherent recognition that it is ultimately language that constructs and deconstructs our notions of identity:

> … reality as we perceive it is always profoundly informed by the words we use. And these words carry *several* meanings … poetry's primary fidelity is to language as an interminable metamorphosis of conflicting identities.[13]

Of particular interest to me, however, is not just human and cultural parentage but educational parentage. Education's identity, who and where it comes from as well as the kind of language it uses, profoundly influences education's self-identity. Because of its intimacy with the poetic, education's capacity to remember itself is at risk in this critical moment also. Paradoxically it is in this ancient moment of crisis that what I believe to be an educational identity crisis today has its source also. Education on this island is at risk of forgetting the bigger picture of who and what is its sponsoring ancestry. It has swapped a version of the parent story for what is primarily one slant on a Greek grand narrative of that story. No matter how valuable that Greek version, it is not and cannot serve as education's whole story today since education's parentage is not a one-sided affair. But this ancient *reamhsceál* is also a critical resource for dealing with that educational identity crisis – for now. I say 'for now' because questions of identity are in constant need of renegotiation in the light of changing circumstances and because of identity's roots in language, which is itself always in transition. In this *reamhsceál*, we have a story of two young students accepting a commission from the poets to seek something vital that is in danger of being lost to the community. They depart and it is in the darkness that the search ultimately finds what it is looking for, finds what was in danger of being lost. It is as a result of entering the darkness in which Fergus appears that education, as represented by the young student, can help restore the community's identity, its 'self', to itself and with it education's self to its educational self. This *reamhsceál* or fore-story to the *Táin*, I believe, offers an original Celtic image of education as entering darkness and therefore may offer counterbalance to the Greek image of education as leading towards light.

The two young students, like the students of the bardic schools, have separated from their relatives, affirming in the process the importance of what Heaney has called '... the sense of crossing out from security into the aloneness of your own being ...',[14] still echoed in the experience of each new quota of four- and five-year-olds, each first of September. This separation is significant – Emaine and Muirgen distance themselves, literally, from the familial, from the father and grandfather. This does not mean that the family and the wider community have no role in the educational process. On the contrary, in the image offered here, there is a poetic–prophetic intergenerational responsibility to assemble, to reflect on the situation of society, to read the signs of the times, to identify as far as possible what is lacking and to offer a commission, 'which of you in return for my/our blessing ... ', a commission that is taken up by the young students of the next generation. What the story and the young students model is a voluntary acceptance of being 'sent out' by one's family and one's community to seek that which one's community is in critical need of, i.e. narrative restoration or the remembering of the community's critical story or stories. Education as modelled in this image is about searching in the dark for the re-storying of the community and of the individual and in the process the re-storying of education itself.

It is a journey that one does not undertake alone, but acknowledges the company of others. Yet, while much of the journey is made in others' company, at its critical point, the students separate again, suggesting that although much that is educational may be a collective experience, at critical junctures it must be solitary. It is an undertaking which is not aimless – Emaine and Muirgen have been pointed in a general direction courtesy of the community's wisdom and memory, but they must also discover as they go along where it is they are going or, as Theodore Roethke says in *The Waking*, 'I learn by going where I have to go'. This is in contrast or counterbalance to the kind of Greek knowing in advance where one is to go and to lead others, i.e. to look at the fixed reality that is the sun, the Good, and proceed in that direction. Neither is it just a matter of education's or the student's conscious control of the searching process; it is a matter of ceding at least a degree of control to events so that one is overtaken by circumstances. For example, Emaine and the others make preparations to 'manage' the darkness that overtakes the students. They go looking for a house for the night. The others having left him, Muirgen sits down beside the gravestone and allows himself to be overtaken, or 'taken over', by night, by darkness. Knowing how to respond to circumstances and signs along the way is a learning in-the-moment which cannot be pre-planned or pre-scripted. It is also significant that, while the whole company comes across the gravestone of Fergus mac Róich, Muirgen alone 'sat down at Fergus' gravestone' and entered into conversation with it, 'as though it were Fergus himself'. The act of 'sitting down with' is in itself a significant educational process; sitting down and spontaneous entering into conversation with the symbolic – in this case a stone – is a primary and committed act of imagining. A willingness to sit down with and enter imaginatively into conversation with what one meets along life's way is critical to this educational process.

Fergus's gravestone is a significant marker, not an actual, historical stone; its importance is symbolic. It marks the boundary between the actual and the possible in the narrative, between the oral and the written, the remembered and the forgotten, between Muirgen's world and an other-world. But although, on the one hand, it represents the mystery beyond, on the other hand, its realism is as concrete as stone. As such it is an apt symbol in itself for the role of poetry and its writing process in education, given that poetry in the public perception is considered 'outside the current of normal life' and yet it is quite concretely and simply seen as '... language which consists of the best words, in the best order ...'.[15] The gravestone is another kind of swallow hole in which differing realities meet and mediate. To repeat a phrase used earlier, it is a point of entry and exit for the buried life of feelings (in this case feelings about education) that in reality poetry gains access to and from. And it is poetic language that gains Muirgen access to the darkness, the origin in which memory and identity are voiced, restored and made whole again – at least for the present. The six lines of speech–poetry he chants to the gravestone – 'If this your royal rock / were your own self mac Róich / halted here with sages / searching for a roof / Cualinge we'd recover / plain and perfect Fergus' – act as a kind of spell. The use of this kind of speech–poetry is not uncommon in early sagas like the *Táin*. The form of stories is a combination of prose and verse, the main narrative in prose, while any heightening of the mood is marked by the use of verse, ordinarily so that the poems are spoken by one of the characters. This literary form appears first in ancient India and is perhaps the earliest form of literature known to the Indo-Europeans for whom 'The poetry of the sagas ... is an artistic device used with great effect to increase the emotional power of the prose narrative'.[16] The poetry in the instance of the saga in question is not just a device that heightens mood, however; it is a manifestation of the ancient links between art and sorcery, between chant and the mantic power of spells, charms and curses; a link that required 'direct speech' if potential power were to be realised. It bore testimony to the poet as a kind of threshold figure standing on the boundary between the here-and-now and the elsewhere-and-when, that aforementioned 'power-point' through which non-usual power passes back and forth, but more importantly through which this world and the other-world (the world beyond what I have been calling the 'factual-actual') kept in communication. That communication is conducted 'by ear', by an aural and oral process of listening in, and sounding out. In the heightened mood created by the voice, the strong pattern and solid rhythmic emphases of the chant knock, metaphorically, on Fergus mac Róich's gravestone, like a series of dull, thudding, sound-signals.[17]

It is as though from its own depths, the primitive audial memory of the race picks up the pattern of what it hears on the surface as Muirgen's words strike the gravestone; it gathers and directs a physical momentum of sound-waves and issues forth a current of syntactical (in the sense of syntax as 'constitution of body') force that finds expression in the bodily appearance of Fergus. Fergus arrives before Muirgen like an arrow in the dark to its target. The teacher who is sensitive to the poetic represents a similar kind of power-point: one who stands at the junction of communications between an educational world (paraphrasing Heaney) given over to the adequacy of a socio-technical response to life and an educational world which would seek out the world-renewing potential of the imagined response to life.[18] The poetic in this way fosters a heightened sensitivity in an education system which tends for the most part to be prose-bound and sight-bound, and would nourish education's capacity to 'release pupils from imprisonment in the essay form and from passive repetition of other people's ideas'.[19] These six lines of poetic chant act as a sound-symbol, a summoning of the energies of words, embodying in the person of Fergus the way in which poetry opens up education's access to critical resources with which to explore vaster, deeper realities and to remember them in the present.

Fergus, being an exile (from Ulster), is the appropriate one to appear out of the past and represent, not the one-sided certainties of the heroic Cúchulainn or Maeve one might have expected to meet, but the rich ambivalence of divided loyalty and conflicting identities (as did Hector too). Being an exile, Fergus retained some sense of loyalty to Ulster and took discreet steps, at various points in the saga, to assist his former people. He, therefore, was the only one with *experiential* access to both sides of the story. Fergus represents the necessity which Ivan Illich believed to be of central importance for education and educators, that of *questioning one's certainties*, another name for one's loyalties or for our collective Grand Narratives. Muirgen represents an attitude that is open to such possibilities. He does not, like the others in his company, seek shelter from the darkness, but remains open to possibilities contained within it. But openness to possibilities, particularly those that are hidden in darkness, without the necessary resources to explore those possibilities, is, as the ollamh of the bardic school knew, pointless. And just as they offered their students certain rules, forms, rituals and practices for working in the dark, so too as apprentice-poet Muirgen was sufficiently resourceful, sufficiently attuned to poetry's ways, means and rhythms to follow it instinctively. He was sufficiently skilled in the mechanics of poetry to craft a chant or password that would allow him to enter the dark. It is through entering the dark space and time (the traditional three days and three nights) in which he is 'lost' to those around him, that Muirgen, the representative student, finds Fergus a critical source of the whole story, or at least a version of 'the whole story'. Fergus's negotiation of divided loyalty/certainty/identity allowed him, and only him, to restore a version of the story and with it a version of the people's identity. The story of the search for and the finding of Fergus' story may allow the possibility of searching Ted Hughes' vast system of root-meanings and related associations, deep in the subsoil of (education's) psychological life, beyond our immediate awareness or conscious manipulation today. In the process, the negotiating and questioning of today's educational certainties and loyalties may help to restore an as-well-as-Greek philosophical version of Irish education's identity, for the present.

Apart from his role as questioner of loyalty and identity, and teller of the whole story, there is an added significance to the fact that it is Fergus whom one meets at this point of origin. Fergus was one of the foster-parents (it was customary for those of high rank to have several different foster-parents) to Cúchulainn, one of the main characters in the *Táin*. In substituting so intimately for the parent, the foster-parent played a role similar to the wet-nurse, a role that also carried educational responsibilities.[20] Fergus, as foster-father, and the nurse from the previous chapter, both embody education charged with a nourishing–rearing function. Consequently, the fortunes of Hector's son and Senchán's son contrast in that the former is taken from the nurse/educator, while the other ends up in the foster-parent/educator's company. An important contrast also exists between Hector's perception of his society's needs and their influence, through him, on the life of his son, and Senchán's perception of his society's needs and their influence on the life of his son. With differing senses of authority, Hector faces himself and his son towards the light of the future and the blessings of the immortal gods; Senchán orientates himself and his son towards the past and the darkness and the story-keeper and offers his own blessing to his son. Hector's son is subjected to 'the Greek will to force' whereas Senchán's son volunteers and, with his father's blessing, explores and reconnects himself as individual, and his people, via their poet-collective, with the unconscious of the whole race. In his role as poet–teacher or 'ollamh', Senchán equips his son with language skills such as composition and the use of chant, which gain him access to that unconscious. Importantly also, Senchán charges his son/pupil with the responsibility of returning eventually with something of value for its citizens, i.e. a strong sense of identity, the linguistic skills of the poet, needed for the ongoing negotiation of that identity and an understanding of education's role in fostering that identity and those skills. It would seem therefore that the Celtic image of education worked with here offers the possibility of redressing the dominance of the Greek image explored earlier, to the benefit of education, its participants – both learners and teachers – and society at large.

That Fergus is described in such detail serves to emphasise his corporeality and consequent authenticity as source or origin. That he is described in such vivid colour – a head of brown hair, in a green cloak and a red embroidered hooded tunic, with gold-hilted sword and bronze blunt sandals – suggests that, unlike Plato's cave with its two-dimensional, monochrome shadows, the poetic darkness of the Celtic 'cave' is, in the 'light' by which poetry perceives things, iridescent. (The brown, green, red and in particular the 'blunt bronze' provide an earthedness in contrast to the description of Hector with his helmet flashing and fiery in the sun etc.) This iridescence rewards the faith and trust in language, particularly poetry, that was required before one could gain entry to the dark. But, more significantly, 'learning' is the ultimate blessing-in-return for Muirgen's search in the dark. Muirgen's 'learning' is *a version* of *'the whole story'*. And it is a blessing not only for Muirgen as individual, but for the whole community, because it is a version of *their* story. Thus, this image of education as entering darkness symbolises the creative tension between language and learning and between the educational needs of the individual and the needs of society. It provides an example not only of restoration of 'the self to the self'[21] that Heaney speaks of, (and a restoration of education's self to itself), but of restoration of the community to the community. Muirgen remembers the community, for now. It seems to me that this encounter is the point of origination and restoration of poetry's role in, and as a model of, education. It is this encounter that images education as a movement from light into darkness rather than from darkness to light.

The archetypal image of education as entering darkness found its corporeality, its embodiment, in Ireland in the famous Bardic schools. Like the young apprentice poets Muirgen and Emaine, apprentice poets of the bardic schools headed off at the darkest time of each year, when days were shortest and nights longest. Such is the significance and importance of the educational process of these schools that it is worth quoting at length from a description of them found in the Memoirs of the Marquis of Clanricarde published in 1722, a description of a process which had probably gone on unchanged for centuries before the coming of Christianity:

> The Professors (one or more as there was occasion) gave a Subject suitable to the Capacity of each class, determining the number of Rhimes and clearing what was to be chiefly observed therein as to Syllables, Quartans, Concord, Correspondence, Termination

and Union, each of which were restrained by peculiar rules. The said Subject (either one or more as aforesaid) having been given over Night, they worked at it apart each by himself upon his own Bed, the whole next Day in the Dark, till at a certain Hour in the Night, Lights being brought in, they committed it to writing.[22]

Students spent as many as twelve years studying in the bardic schools.[23] The schools operated during the autumn and winter months and darkness became a necessary condition for the kind of 'languaged-learning' poetry and its writing process modelled. Although students were encouraged to work in the dark they were not abandoned to the darkness. They were given strict instructions and guidelines on how to work within it, establishing a process that deserves remembering and reconsidering – if not reconfiguring – in education today. Today's students must also be given guidance on how to work in the dark, not only the students of language, literature and the arts but students of the sciences too. After all, when one comes to the limits of one's scientific knowledge one finds oneself ultimately 'in the dark'; darkness vastly outsizes light in our universe. How to work when one is at the limits of 'the known' is a question of imaginative educational processes that reach into the darkness of that condition and raid the inarticulate. The processes whereby poetry gets made, as the bardic schools knew, have an affinity with such darkness. The nature of this poetry's writing process and the learning it embodies will be examined in detail in subsequent chapters. For now education must remember an ancestry for whom working in the dark was primary.

The bardic schools enjoyed wealthy patronage as well as local support, often in the form of provisions being donated to both students and teachers. A graduate of the schools would become a highly qualified professor of literature, trained in the use of a very sophisticated poetic language, all of which would admit him to an elite class in society. In fact, such was the status of the poet that they often proved a heavy burden for the poor and for patrons, whom they expected to maintain them in a style and fashion reflecting their polished creativity. In an essay entitled *The Concept of an Academy and the Celts* Jorge Luis Borges writes of these schools:

> A literary career required more than twelve years of strict studies, which included mythology, legendary history, topography and law. To such disciplines we must obviously add grammar and the various branches of rhetoric. The teaching was oral, as it is with all esoteric material; there were no written texts, and the student had to commit to memory the entire *corpus* of the earlier literature. The annual examination lasted many hours; the student, kept in a dark cell and provided with food and water, had to versify certain set genealogical and mythological subjects in certain set meters and then memorise them. The lowest grade, that of *oblaire,* was given for poems on seven subjects; the highest grade, *ollam,* for 360, corresponding to the days in the lunar year ... If the concept of an academy is based on the organisation and direction of literature, then there was no more academic country, not even France or China.[24]

It is important to note, however, that the 'graduates' of the bardic school would not necessarily become poets; graduates would take up roles ranging in scope from the prophetic to the editorial, observing and commenting on the signs of the times. Their comments and opinions would be sought after and highly regarded. Whether or not the graduate of the bardic school turned out to be a great poet depended not only on his having learned his craft, but also on whether he had the gift of poetry. The bardic schools did not simply, or singly, have the creation of poets as their aim; particularly significant was their emphasis on the role of poetry and its writing process in their unique education system and consequently their fosterage of the relationship between the oral, the aural and the darkness.[25] Not since the decline of these schools has education taken poetry pedagogically or professionally to heart.

It has been suggested that the roots of the bardic educational process's emphasis on darkness lay in some pre-Christian, druidic rite or ceremony; indeed, in the literature, the words '*filí*' and '*druí*' are often interchangeable. But the roots of the emphasis on darkness may also be linked to poetry's closer affinity with the ear than with the eye and to that kind of poetic blindness[26] which renders one undistracted and thereby able to see further into the heart of the matter. It is also important to remember lest it be over-romanticised that, with regard to the high social standing of the graduate of the bardic school, it

> was in no small degree due to careful cultivation of it by the poets themselves. It suited them to be regarded as indispensable to the culture, as in a special way embodying the very spirit of the culture itself, and so they spoke much of their profession and disseminated a large body of lore concerning famous practitioners of the art ... That the poets continued to boast of their trade as something apart is clear from literature down through the ages.[27]

It was not unusual that a primitive society would be eager to hold in high esteem people whose talents were understood to be supernatural. The poet, like the Christian cleric and the Jewish prophet, was believed to mediate between this world and the other-world, between the realm of humanity and the realm of the gods. The poet was a kind of two-way power-point. This power-point existed unquestioned, even after the coming of a rival power – Christianity – to Ireland. After all, the coming of the first Christian clerics to Ireland may not have presented any immediate crisis of faith and choice of loyalty for the ordinary citizen, since, for a pantheistic society, what's another god? For a considerable period after the coming of Christianity and Graeco-Roman influence to Ireland, the language of poetry was still associated with '*dorchacht*, darkness, the strange almost indecipherable language in which the poets conversed with one another'.[28] The language of Christianity, on the other hand, was often referred to as the 'white language', with its emphasis on Christ the Light of the world. But in the early days of Christianity in Ireland the white and the dark languages co-existed, contrary to popular belief. In the socio-religious and educational realms of that time, the *ollamh* and the *easpag* were of similar standing. And, although differences did exist between lay and monastic schools, they too happily co-existed.[29] It is significant that along with this period of 'creative tension' between images and languages of light and darkness there came – if only for a century or two – a powerful period of Celtic educational influence throughout Europe. It was a period when the socio-religious and educational spheres came to inhabit what Celan calls 'the frontiered limbo between light and darkness', in which 'he speaks truly who speaks the shade'.[30] However, the balance proved difficult to sustain.[31] Although the two school systems of the time – the monastic and the lay bardic – had Latin and Greek Grammar on their curricula, the monastic concentrated on Scripture's 'white language', while the lay bardic schools concentrated on poetry's dark language. The eventual Romanisation of the

Irish monasteries in the thirteenth century narrowed the support base of literature in the vernacular, forcing it into the patronage of prominent Gaelic families, thus making bardic poets, their poetry and their schools more of an elite than ever before.

The beginning of the bardic education system is impossible to date; it was already ancient when St Patrick came to Ireland in the fifth century and it lasted for centuries afterwards. Its eventual collapse is usually attributed to the collapse of its remaining support system, the old Gaelic order, after the Flight of The Earls in 1607. But the collapse of that Gaelic order may in a psychic sense be as much an effect as a cause. The poets of the bardic era had, as Ó hÓgáin reminded us, a vested interest in things cultural remaining as they were. In his book *Inventing Ireland,* Declan Kiberd suggests in a chapter entitled 'The National Longing for Form'[32] that at the turn of this present century the 'cultural renaissance preceded by many years the declaration of political independence'. In other words, life imitated art. Life however, may also have imitated art with regard to the collapse of the Gaelic order. It is as though the extended era of the bardic schools provided an example, not of 'national longing for form', but a restricted, elitist form of national longing. That form was intricately bound up with the strict, elitist nature of bardic poetry,[33] which in its linguistic structure and in the cultivated status of its practitioners failed to foster emergent forms of poetic challenge that might have translated into new forms of political and cultural life. It was as though a restricted, elitist linguistic form stifled life. It was language for language's sake and eventually that language tradition imploded.

Removed from what was in the early period of Irish Christianity a creative tension between native tradition and Christianity, between images of darkness and light[34] and remote from the life, needs, interests and language of the ordinary citizen, it was at this point that the Undine's freedom began to turn cold and aloof. The stream of poetic consciousness, its image and its educational influence, very rapidly disappeared underground:

> When the change came, it came suddenly. The old Gaelic world went to pieces and numbers of highly trained, educated men found that their once honourable profession had disappeared ... While it lasted they were held in honour. Neither they nor their patrons dreamed that a change was needed ...[35]

In terms of the image and story in this chapter, it is as though Muirgen, the representative of future generations, remained steadfastly in the dark mist conversing with Fergus; visited the 'origin' but failed to return to his community, thereby frustrating the future. In this respect, the bardic era offers a cautionary tale for an education that would over-indulge the poetic. Indeed any language – including that technical language that predominates in educational discourse today – that distances itself from the speech of ordinary people may suffer the same consequences as the bardic schools.

The most important educational consequence of the collapse of the bardic schools, however, was that the links between language, learning and the role of poetry and its writing process in education also collapsed. A creative tension or counterbalance capable of counter-pointing the image, process and language of education as leading out towards light was unavailable and education has suffered the consequences. Although the study of poetry continues to be part of education down to the present day, not since then has the hands-on composition of poetry been as influential in the school curriculum nor has it 'modelled' a way of learning, an overarching educational process. The image of education as 'entering darkness' lost its influence; the Undine went underground, became unconscious, ceded right of way to the Greek image whose orientation towards light allowed for its natural alliance with Christianity, its symbolism and its ideological battles with the powers of darkness, down the centuries. Devoid of poetic counterbalance after the decline of the bardic schools, Church and State education, though they may have had different aims, were both essentially phototropic in direction. They were interested in educational practice as *techne*, as a means to achieving a preconceived end in terms of mastery of the individual's nature – body and/or soul – usually by the mastery of language in the form of rote learning. In the process, mastery of educational discourse followed suit. Thus in its religious and in its general forms, primary education's process and language led out of darkness towards light.

The challenge to this book is to imitate the action of the digger and to restore the Undine's right of way through education's channels; to take account of poetry's role in life and in learning, to link poetry in education to society in a way that the bardic schools did for so long, but also to learn the lesson of an overly independent 'cold freedom'. It is to remember that the circle was not complete until the students returned to their awaiting community, told the story and the awaiting community rejoiced. At the heart of the matter of education today lies a situation exactly like that which faced Senchán centuries ago, i.e. a fragmented memory of education's 'parentage' and the suppression of poetic influence renders educators unable to give account of or tell 'our whole educational story'. Education's orientation to the modern day 'white language' of technical rationalism renders it unable to gain access to that 'darkness', in which lies the possibility of reconnecting with a vital origin in the past. Furthermore, education today does not speak the language of narrative; it is incapable of telling educators even a version of a story which they can understand and so recognise themselves, remember who they are. Senchán, the *ollamh*, faced a challenge like that which faces teachers today, i.e. to foster the search for (a version of) education's whole story. We need to restore poetic influence to education so that we have access to a way of *voicing,* of giving account and having account taken, of who we are, where we have come from, what we are doing and how.

I have sought to rehabilitate a Celtic image of education into the story of our educational past as a way of counterbalancing our Greek educational parentage. In reconnecting education today with an important source or origin of poetic consciousness I believe I may in the process have – by accident or gift – come across a gravestone of my own and restored something of my own teaching-self to itself also. It is as though, having fallen down the swallow hole in the poem 'Undine', traipsed around after the two young apprentice poets, and entered the darkness with Muirgen, one of my own ancestors 'appeared' and something of the story of my own origins in teaching was restored; an origin below certification and qualification, below conscious levels of thought and feeling. It is an origin I gained access to by way of another personal 'early orphaned memory' and I recount it here as an example of re-storying one's own teaching self.

Mac an Fhir Léinn

My grandfather lived on a small farm a hundred yards or so down the road from our house, a distance that divided life in 'the new houses' from 'the tail-end of his steadier way of life that had persisted right through from medieval times'.[36] Every so often while my older brothers and sisters were at school he would dander up the road at his retired leisure to visit my mother and me. He laboured up some rough steps hewn out of the bank, a short-cut residents had created to circumvent the longer but official route into the estate. He walked along the path, through our gate, around the house and came in the back door.

He never came empty handed. His 'old clothes' – trousers, jumper, dungarees, waistcoat and jacket – were a labyrinth of cavernous pockets. Deep in among these pockets, farm-fresh eggs straight from the hen-house were hidden as secretly as if, unknown even to him, wise old hens had laid them there. He sat down, opened his penknife, cut his Warhorse Plug tobacco and his wink was my signal to 'Go!' While the kettle boiled, the two of us played our ritual game. I inserted my hand – and most of the length of my small arm – into his various pockets in search of their hidden contents. Fingers became 'eyes-out-on-sticks', urgent and expectant, feeling their excited way around the deep dark depths. The large pocket on the bib of the dungarees was always a bit too obvious but a good place to start. From there I covered the whole course – trouser pockets, coat pockets, inside pockets, outside pockets, and all other secret pockets in between. I always saved the best till last, my favourite pocket, the long skinny one down the side of the dungarees, designed to hold a carpenter's ruler. Blindly I guessed at shapes, estimated sizes, I figured, or 'fingered' out what I encountered there – tobacco box, bottle-opener, matches, hanky, string, assorted nails and screws, one or two coins – gradually getting the measure of those light-less spaces as one by one they yielded their hidden-most secret. One by one each egg was 'found out'. One by one each en-shelled little world, weighted and measured and nestled in the palm of my hand, each completely the 'full of itself' as was the child who discovered it, surrendered and gave itself up to its destiny. The old man spoke very little, but smiled at each new find in this game which only ended when half a dozen eggs were duly accounted for and sat like obedient pupils in a row on the kitchen table. That ritual complete, my mother would begin another. She boiled three eggs, buttered bread, wet tea and we tucked in. When his visit had been paid and received in full, my mother – anxious about his increasing frailty – linked him down the steps, down the bank and set him safely on his road home again.

I stumbled across this memory as I stumbled around in the darkness, following Muirgen. Having entered into conversation with it through the writing process, I bring it back to the surface with me and I now rejoice because I realise that this game, searching in the depths of those dark pockets, was for me 'an emblem of initiation, like putting your hand into the bush or robbing the nest, one of the various natural analogies for uncovering and touching the hidden thing'.[37] My grandfather's name was McErlean which may be translated as son of the man of Learning. He represented the figure of the *mac an fhir léinn*, wise old '*senex*' or '*ollamh*'. He was like an assemblage of deep pockets of quiet learning, a representative of our own educational-wisdom. It was he, I believe, who inducted me into teaching, into education as entering darkness and perhaps even commissioning me to remember education's story in this book. It was he in a sense who commissioned me to search and find and bring something back out into the broad daylight, something that would nourish us all. The eggs, symbol of new life, were 'blessing in return'. The ritual 'meal' celebrated the life-renewing potential of the 'age-old'; of myth and tradition and ritual itself. For the teacher to become aware of his or her own small educational story vibrating off the bigger collective educational myth, is for him or her to become a kind of tuning fork making solid narrative contact with the educational ground under one's pedagogic feet. It is then to be in a position to emit an educational note, divined in the depths of the larger tradition but emitted in a unique personal voice. To find a version of one's own and one's community's educational parent-story is to find the voice with which to tell – at least for now – *an authentic version* of a story that is in danger of being forgotten.

I and my poet-guide emerge out of these remembrances into the landscape, to find the young boy and the digger watching:

> the way the water in the cleared-out place, as soon as the shovelfuls of sludge had been removed, the way the water began to run free, rinse itself clean of the soluble mud and make its own little channels and currents.[38]

As I too watched, it struck me that the challenge in restoring the teacher's voice is the challenge of doing the spade work that will allow education's waters to begin to run free, to rinse itself clean and to make its own little channels and currents in today's world. It is the challenge of researching, remembering *other than* the now overgrown version of our educational parent story. One line of our educational topology, genealogy and identity is being forgotten and with it the poetic stream that could foster the 'restoryation' of itself to itself. In the overgrown version, education's narrative arteries are clogged – not that education, especially primary education, does not tell stories: no section of the education system tells more stories. But while education *tells* stories, it does not generate and regenerate *its own story*; it doesn't 'story itself'. To tell and re-tell our own stories is to begin to recreate and regenerate an educational culture in which story and poetic language is recognised and legitimated – not just as 'anecdotal evidence' supporting this or that theory but as *an imaginative way of knowing*. Because it does not re-story itself, our experience as educators is schlerosed; it hardens into analysis, concepts, abstractions, all of which lead to a kind of 'theoretical obesity' in education. And yet the teacher, the classroom, the playground and the staffroom are breeding grounds for stories – intimate stories, funny stories, sad stories, small stories of little apparent consequence, life stories like the one Carolyn Steedman tells as she looks back on her time as a teacher:

> We stayed together in one room most of the day long. Shabby, depressed, disturbed, social-priority children learned to read under my care; the efficacy of affection. I admired their stoicism under disaster; I lost my temper with them; they longed for my approval again. I could silence a room with a glance. I was good at jokes, the raised eyebrow, the smile, the delicate commentary on the absurdity of things that is the beginning of irony in eight year olds. We laughed a lot, wept over all the sad stories. An on-going show of human variety ... classrooms are places of gossip, places for the observation of infinite change: new shoes, new haircuts, a pair of gold ear-rings for pierced ears; passion, tears, love, despair ...

Classrooms are a million stories in themselves. 'In telling their own stories, cultures, [including educational culture] create themselves ...'[39] Story is how we make sense of being teachers or pupils. Narration is how we tell, and therefore come to know and understand poetically, who we are as teachers, what we are doing and why we are doing it. Story is how we make our own little channels and currents in education and in life. In finding, remembering and searching again for our individual and collective educational story, however minute or mythical, we rediscover the teacher-voice with which we must begin to tell it – *out loud.*

Notes

1. Steiner comments on this idea of abundance of language in relation to social class: 'The privileged speak to the world at large as they do to themselves, in a conspicuous consumption of syllables, clauses, prepositions, concomitant with their economic resources and the spacious quarters they inhabit. Men and women of the lower class do not speak to their masters and enemies as they do to one another, hoarding what expressive wealth they have for internal use.' *After Babel*, p. 34. The same may be said in relation to the powerful and less-powerful classes within education, I believe.
2. Heaney, *Door into the Dark*, London, Faber, 1969, p. 26.
3. Ibid.
4. McGrath, F., *Education in Ancient and Medieval Ireland*, Studies 'Special Publications', p. 37.

   'All recent scholars, however, have emphasised the wide and varied scope of these functions [i.e. the functions of the *Filí*]. The Filid were guardians of the ancient traditions, history, topography, epics, pedigrees, laws. They were advisors of rulers, witnesses of contracts. By their satires they governed the social conscience. Their knowledge of genealogies was relied on to establish or maintain territorial rights. By their appeal to past glories they stimulated national pride or martial ardour. They held a recognised place in the social structure ...'
5. Heaney says of this poem: 'I once said it was a myth about agriculture, about the way water is tamed and humanised when streams become irrigation canals, when water becomes involved with seed.' *Preoccupations*, p. 54. I interpret it in an edu-cultural sense.
6. Ibid.
7. Heaney, *New Selected Poems*, London, Faber, 1990, p. 9.
8. *Preoccupations*, p. 53.
9. See *Seamus Heaney Fiftieth Birthday Issue*, Agenda Editions Charitable Trust, 1989, p. 26.
10. Sometimes referred to as 'The Irish Iliad'.
11. Ibid., pp. 1–2. Another version of the same story can be found in Flower's *The Irish Tradition*, Oxford, Clarendon Press, 1947.
12. Dillon, M., *Early Irish Literature*, Dublin, Four Courts Press, 1948, p. 2.
13. Kearney, R., *Transitions: Narratives In Modern Irish Culture*, Dublin, Wolfhound Press, p. 103.

14. Heaney in interview with John Quinn in *My Education*, Dublin, Townhouse in assoc. with RTÉ, p. 167.
15. See Bullock Report, 9.22, p. 135.
16. *Early Irish Literature*, p. 150.
17. Ted Hughes in an Afterword to *The School Bag*, London, Faber, 1997, illuminates the 'mechanics' of this process: '... verbal sounds are organically linked to the vast system of root meanings and related associations, deep in the subsoil of psychological life, beyond our immediate awareness or conscious manipulation. It is the distinction of poetry to create strong patterns in these hidden meanings as well as in the clearly audible sounds. The hidden patterns are, if anything, much the stronger. The audial memory picks up those patterns in the depth from what it hears at the surface ... We feel them almost as a physical momentum of inevitability, a current of syntactical force purposefully directed like the flight of an arrow in the dark.' It seems to me that this describes the process by which Muirgen's chant acted on the hard surface of reality to evoke the appearance of Fergus, and the voicing of his story, deep below.
18. *The Redress of Poetry;* Heaney's actual comment is that 'in the end the poem is more given over to the extraordinary than to the ordinary, more dedicated to the world renewing potential of the imagined response than to the adequacy of the social one'. p. xvii.
19. Cox, B., *Cox on Cox: An English Curriculum for the 1990s*, London, Hodder and Stoughton, 1991, p. 80.
20. 'The laws distinguish two types of fosterage. One is fosterage for affection *(altrann serce)* for which no fee is paid. The other type of fosterage is for a fee ... The foster-parents are required to maintain their foster-child according to his or her rank ... The foster-child must also be educated in accordance with his or her rank.' Kelly, F., *A Guide to Early Irish Law*, Dublin Institute for Advanced Studies, 1995.
21. *Preoccupations*, p. 41.
22. Bergin, O., *Irish Bardic Poetry*, Dublin Institute for Advanced Studies, 1970, p. 5.
23. Declan Kiberd gives the following description in a chapter entitled 'Beckett's Texts of Laughter and Forgetting':
    'The process of composition was carried out by the Gaelic *filí* as they lay on pallets in small, darkened rooms. This dark seclusion protected them from distracting light and noise and recalled the ancient links between art and sorcery. To secure

themselves further, some of the poets lay with stones on their bellies or in the hands ... or even with plaids around their heads ... The subject of a bardic exercise was set overnight: the *filí* worked on it all day, each lying on his bed in the dark until night fell, when at last lights were brought in and the words written down.' *Inventing Ireland: The Literature of the Modern Nation*, London, Vintage, 1995, p. 536.

24. 'The poems were classified by themes: destructions of lineages or castles, thefts of animals, loves, battles, sea voyages, violent deaths, expeditions, kidnappings and fires. Other categories included visions, attacks, plots, certain meters and a certain vocabulary to which the poet was limited under penalty of punishment. For the highest poets, versification was extremely complex, and included assonance, rhyme and alliteration. Rather than direct reference, they preferred an intricate system of metaphors, based on myth or legend or personal invention.' See 'The Concept of an Academy and the Celts' in *Jorge Luis Borges: Selected Non-Fictions*, Eliot Weinberger (ed.) London, Penguin Books, 1999, p. 458.

25. Corkery, D., in *The Hidden Ireland*, Dublin, Gill and MacMillan, 1924, says, 'Whatever may have been the relative positions of the monkish schools and those of the bards, the latter, all authorities agree, were the university system of the nation ... In Europe of the Dark and Middle Ages the universities were frankly Church institutions ... In Ireland, on the other hand, the bardic schools which obviously exerted great influence in the nation's life were a repository of learning and were, at the same time, frankly a lay institution ... one searches Europe in vain for the equivalent of our bardic school system ...'

26. Borges, *In Praise of Darkness*, p. 478.

27. Ó hÓgáin, D., *The Hero in Irish Folk History*, Dublin, Gill and Macmillan, 1985, p. 217.

28. Ó hÓgáin writes of this poetic language: '"dorchacht" [darkness] – a cryptic language which the poets used to talk to each other. Another term for it was "iarmbérla" which the ninth century glossary of Cormac mac Cuilennáin explains in the following way ... It is called that because of the dimness of the language and because of its darkness and condensation, so that it is not easy to decipher it ... Obviously it was a kind of meta-language and given the magical powers attributed to poets and poetry in ancient Ireland it too was understood to belong to the

other-world. Respect for this language is a very ancient thing with parallels in other Indo-European cultures.' Ibid.

29. An example of their co-existence: 'Though differing in aim there does not appear to have been any actual antagonism between them. They were to a large extent complementary ... On one occasion, it is recorded, they inquired from the Saint [Columba/Colmcilole] why he did not ask an Irish poet who visited Iona to recite a poem for them after the seroman – a question that did not scandalise the saint in the least ... These examples are given for the purposes of removing a false impression that there was a clear-cut line of demarcation between the study of native and classical literature.' Graham, H., *The Early Irish Monastic Schools*, Dublin, Talbot Press, 1923, p. 236.

30. See Kearney, R., *The Wake of Imagination: Toward A Postmodern Culture*, London, Routledge, 1994, p. 122.

31. Whereas many of the native Irish saints such as Colmcille managed to interweave a mystical, indulgent love of nature with religious self-denial and an austere lifestyle, St Patrick may have a case to answer in tipping the contrast balance from darkness towards light since of 'the three qualifications of a poet – *imbas forosna, teinm laída* and *díchetal di chennaib* – St Patrick forbade the practice of *imbas forosna* and *teinm laída* because they were incompatible with Christianity. With regard to *díchetal di chennaib,* however ... the saint allowed that because it comes from ordinary human creativeness and "no offering to demons is necessary". This phrase ... suggests that these aspects of the poetic craft had such a nature.' *The Hero in Irish Folk History*, p. 61.

Two key historians of the period, Knott and Murphy, seem to relieve St Patrick of *personal* responsibility:

'If we were to point to one fact that changed the whole development of literature in Ireland, we would, I think, point to the monastic reform initiated by the Cistercians in the twelfth century. Up to this point the monasteries had been a mainstay of literary production in the vernacular. After this period it is almost as if the monasteries cleaned their cupboards of secular or semi-secular manuscripts, bringing the monks back with a jolt to things more closely connected with salvation than the deeds of Cú Chulainn. From this period on the guardianship of the manuscript remains of early Irish literature, as well as the continuation of productivity in this field, falls increasingly on the great Irish literary families who, quite suddenly, came into prominence about the thirteenth century.' Op. cit. *Early Irish Literature*, Intro.

32. *Inventing Ireland*, p. 117.

33. Knott and Murphy detail the structure of the *'dan díreach'* metre as follows – the first line of each couplet has eight syllables; the second line has seven; the last word of the eight-syllabled line has two syllables; the last word of the seven-syllabled line has three syllables; the end word of the third line rhymes with the penultimate in the last line.

34. Meyer, referring to the fourth–sixth centuries points out that: 'when Christianity came with the authority of Rome and in the Latin language, now imbued with an additional sanctity, there ensued in all nations a struggle between the vernacular and the foreign tongue for obtaining the rank of a literary language ... In Ireland on the other hand, which had received her Christianity not direct from Rome but from Britain and Gaul, and where the Church, far removed from the centre of Roman influence and cut off from the rest of Christendom, was developing on national lines, vernacular literature received a fresh impulse from the new faith ... The national language was employed not only for the purposes of instruction and devotion ... but also in religious prose and poetry, and, still more remarkably, in learned writings ... Her [Ireland's] sons, carrying Christianity and a new humanism over Great Britain and the Continent, became the teachers of whole nations, the counsellors of kings and emperors. For once, if but for a century or two, the Celtic spirit dominated a large part of the Western world, and Celtic ideals imparted a new life ... until they succumbed, not altogether to the benefit of mankind, before a mightier system – that of Rome.' Meyer, K., *Selections From Ancient Irish Poetry*, London, Constable and Co., 1928, p. viii.

35. *Irish Bardic Poetry*, p. 18.

36. Heaney, *My Education*, p. 166.

37. *Preoccupations*, p. 42.

38. Ibid., p. 53.

39. In Kearney, R., *Poetics of Imagining: Modern to Post-modern*, New York, Fordham University Press, 1998, Intro.

3 Teaching from the Boat

To date I have explored Greek and Celtic edu-cultural heritages with their images of education as leading out – whether towards the light or into darkness – and education as a nourishing/fostering. I have begun by groping my way into these images, searching them like the pockets of my grandfather's coats, for what they might contain that would nourish a deeper, more poetic understanding of education and of the teacher. But there is a third influence in my educational heritage. In this third chapter I turn my attention to that pocket in Irish primary education's overcoat that is the Judeo-Christian tradition. Significantly, the Judeo-Christian is already a hyphenated affair, an indication perhaps of its capacity to live with the other, including the Greek and the Celtic. Perhaps it can mediate between these ancestors. In an educational context today religious education is also a hyphenated affair – religion being included in the general primary school curriculum but as separate from it.[1] But even if religion in its contemporary Judeo-Christian form is seen to be separate from the main body of curriculum, the extent to which it has already inlaid, overlaid and under-laid our western cultural and educational heritage is undeniable. Similarly, although traditionally religion is taught between the Angelus bell and the lunch bell, the extent to which the teacher separates herself as 'religion teacher' from herself as 'teacher' is less easily distinguishable. To explore the influence of the educational tradition that is Judeo-Christianity on what we who are primary teachers do, how we do it – at whatever time of the day – and who, in a newly multi-cultural society, we do it with is not therefore a straightforward business. My intention in exploring it is not so that I may 'sort it all out', distinguish religious from secular or civic, segregate – or even integrate – more effectively religion or 'religions' and the general curriculum. To do so would be to assume too much to my conscious – or Greek-thinking – self. In line with the thrust of the two previous chapters, my hope is simply that I may listen in and come to know, in the biblical sense, this Judeo-Christian tradition at work in education presently. Perhaps I can sense the possibility of the Spirit of the Risen Teacher, Jesus, in the educational world in which I operate today, within my classroom, within myself – what St Augustine called 'the teacher within'. Having already listened in and hopefully come to know more of the heart and soul of the Judeo-Christian heritage, I may then speak out of that tradition. Only by being more alert to this Judeo-Christian presence and to those other traditions as co-presences can I work with – and recognise when I work against – their grain. Whether with or against their different grains, that work is carried out in hope, hope in the Havelian sense of a 'state of the soul' that predisposes me, not so much towards '... the expectation that things will turn out successfully but the conviction that something is worth working for, however it turns out'.[2] But how to start or where to begin, that is my immediate problem. No guide has appeared this time to take my hand; I cannot find an obvious door on which to knock. I stand here and look around but nothing 'comes to me'. I don't know where to go; I don't know what to do. I sit down on the ground and take stock.

My travels thus far convince me that the kind of knowledge involved in coming to know the Judeo-Christian tradition at work in education today is primarily a work of imagination, since imagination is a vital element in any profound knowing. To bring knowing into being is, as the Bullock Report noted, 'a formulating process, and language is its ordinary means'. To bring religious knowing into being is equally a formulating process and language is its ordinary means too. Coming to know my Judeo-Christian ancestry will involve an engagement with imagination and with ordinary language. The ordinary and the imagined are interdependent and underwritten by language that is both their air and their breathing. Or, as George Steiner has suggested:

> ... any coherent understanding of what language is and how language performs, ... any coherent account of the capacity of human speech to communicate meaning and feeling is, in the final analysis, underwritten by the assumption of God's presence.[3]

The process of coming to know the Judeo-Christian heritage, the past as resurrected present, the possibility of the Risen Teacher in oneself or in the world of education one inhabits, cannot, my explorations would suggest, be achieved by any Greek-rooted technical–rational or scientific methodology, no matter how sophisticated. It cannot be so because the knowing involved is not technical–rational to begin with. Such methodologies may have an important role to play in different ways, but coming to 'know God' is not the guarantee-able result of a planned campaign of action, no matter how effective, nor can knowledge of God be objectively assessed even with hindsight. On the other hand the Celtic image of Muirgen's encounter in the dark might have more to offer because it has its origins in the *hearing* of an invitation – it issues that invitation on behalf of the assembled community, 'Which of you in return for my blessing …'. It is the story of a response to that call (and in this respect it has biblical undertones). Muirgen's is the story of a process made up of micro-processes, including a desire to remember, a willingness to search, an apprenticeship to language, a capacity to engage with symbols, and a commitment to bring something back to one's sponsoring community. Remembering, inviting–responding, searching for significant stories, returning, rejoicing: these are interesting verbs. They constitute the very grammar of religious education. Religious education must foster or nourish this kind of coming to know, remembering, to begin with, that 'coming' works both ways: it is not always I who make the approach, but that which I desire to know may also come towards me. In this same way, religious education in the primary school must remember its Jewish heritage, invite its young students to search for their identity within the Judeo-Christian story and, in doing so, to re-story their awaiting community. This, I believe, is how religious education today nourishes young children's continuous present and future conditional coming to know God.

So perhaps I should take my cue from my Irish educational ancestry – after all it is not a stranger to the Judeo-Christian. They used to know each other quite well. I stand up and, placing my trust in 'learning by going where I have to go', I start walking. But even having responded to the call and begun the search, I will need hints from the community's collective memory, from tradition, as to where I might search, and I will also need to be nurtured along the way by the provision – divine at least some of the time – of significant signs and dynamic symbols in the 'landscape' of the day and the times in which I work. Like Fergus, I do not know yet what these symbols will be but I trust that I will 'come across them'. But even then have I served sufficient apprenticeship to the art of reading or interpreting signs and symbols, talking to them and gaining entry through them into deeper levels of knowing and meaning, access into the realm of 'religious experience'? Well, like Fergus, I will try to enter into them, imaginatively; I will play it by ear ...

Listening in

To play it by ear is to put one's trust in what T.S. Eliot called the audial imagination. Because of its poetic connections, our Celtic educational heritage has an ancient capacity or talent for playing by ear. An emphasis on the oral–aural is not foreign either to a Jewish religious tradition ear-marked by a God who calls, who speaks, who enters into conversation, who listens who ignores! Yet given the over-emphasis on the eye, the visual image and the texted in our contemporary culture and its education, a term such as 'audial imagination' may itself be barely audible. Something Seamus Heaney refers to in relation to the artistic vocation in *The Redress of Poetry* may have the effect of turning up the sound on what audial imagination is. He quotes Robert Pinsky:

> An artist needs not so much an audience, as to feel a need to answer, a promise to respond. The promise may be a contradiction, it may be unwanted, it may go unheeded ... but it is owed, and the sense that it is owed is a basic requirement for the poet's good feeling about the art.[4]

The feeling of a need to answer, a promise to respond, may not be exactly the same for the artist and the disciple, for the poet–teacher and the prophet–teacher, but neither may it be all that dissimilar, a point that I will return to later. For now it is important to emphasise that the feeling of a need to answer, a promise to respond, is an indication that some signal – 'aural sign' – is already being picked up. Training or, more accurately, 'attuning' the ear to the particular wavelength in which that signal 'broadcasts its secret stations' to society and to the individual is of the essence in a religious education.[5]

The ear and the audial imagination are the critical faculty in the education of a poet but the bardic schools, uniquely, recognised their wider importance for a good education, even if they became overly besotted by it. This was understandable; a risk that goes with the job: they listened to language's sounds and were, like many a narrative seafarer, enchanted. They had not tied themselves to the hard reality of a Greek ship's mast. Recognition of the vital role of the poetic, and the audial imagination in education generally, disappeared with the bardic schools, but now that our educational ship has not only a Greek mast but a Greek wind filling its sails, an ear for the en-*chant*-ments of language, of Word, must be – urgently – restored to education and to religious education today.[6] Some of the pedagogic practicalities of what is involved in attuning the ear will be addressed in the next section of this book, but for now it seems that the way in, the point of entry into the Judeo-Christian tradition, is not by laying it out before myself objectively, 'like a patient etherized upon a table', and by means of edu-surgical operations getting to know it by identifying its various internal organs. The way into the kind of religious 'coming to know' that I am talking about is an active listening-in process, engaging the ear. As I walk along, thinking these thoughts to myself, I remember something else Heaney says. While it is not the development of religious sensibility he has in mind, what he says about William Wordsworth's practice of poetic composition again turns up the sound on guidelines that may offer my walking a direction, something to follow by ear:

Although Wordsworth is here describing the activity of composing aloud, of walking and talking, *what the poetry reaches into is the activity of listening* ... But even though he is listening to the sound of his own voice, he realises that his spoken music is just a shadow of the unheard melody, 'the mind's internal echo'. He is drawn into himself even as he speaks himself out, and it is this mesmerised attention to the echoes and invitations within that constitute his poetic confidence ...

What we are presented with is a version of composition as listening, as a wise passiveness, a surrender to energies that spring within the centre of the mind, not composition as an active pursuit by the mind's circumference of something already at the centre. The more attentively Wordsworth listens in, the more cheerfully and abundantly he speaks out.[7] (my italics)

The capacity for mesmerised attention to echoes and invitations within, to the 'unheard melody' were it nourished in religious education would I believe constitute grounds for religious confidence and composure too. Surely it was the same kind of mesmerised attention to those 'echoes and invitations' within that returned in the voices of Old Testament prophets, such as Jeremiah. Indeed if I may push the comparison a little further, apparently Wordsworth, while he was composing, would pace up and down a path,

the crunch and scuffle of the gravel working like a metre, or a metronome under the rhythms of the ongoing chaunt, those 'trances of thought and mountings of the mind' somehow aided by the automatic, monotonous turns and returns of the walk, the length of the path acting like the length of the line …

We might say, in fact, that Wordsworth at his best is a pedestrian poet. As his poetic feet repeat his footfalls, the earth seems to be a treadmill that he turns; the big diurnal roll is sensed through poetic beat and the world moves like a waterwheel under the fall of his voice.[8]

Wordsworth's habit of pacing up and down, listening in and speaking out as he paced, reminds me of the opening-in and opening-out of the lines in the first verses of the Book of Jeremiah:

The word of Yahweh was addressed to me saying …
I said, 'Ah Lord Yahweh; look, I do not know how to speak …'
Then Yahweh put out his hand and touched my mouth …
The word of Yahweh was addressed to me …
Jeremiah what do you see
I see a branch of the watchful tree …
Then Yahweh said, 'Well seen! …'
A second time the word of Yahweh was spoken to me … what do you see
I see a cooking pot on the boil …
Then Yahweh said, ' … It is Yahweh who speaks.'

It is not difficult to imagine Jeremiah also pacing up and down, his advance and retire, advance and retire, like the readying, steadying and getting set motion that rocks the child back and forward on the spot. This repetitive motion may reflect the motions of Jeremiah's mind – 'Will I? Won't I? Do I? Don't I?' – and all the while 'powers sink in, mould, impress, frame, minister, enter unawares'.[9] Ultimately they find return in the young prophet's expressing 'It is Yahweh who speaks'. Not that this proclamation is the summit, a once and for all achievement; but in these opening lines Jeremiah enters his stride too, finds his rhythm in pacing the paths of the Jewish prophetic tradition and, critically, keeps it going, 'on the boil'.

Finding a voice

A poetic voice like Wordsworth's and a prophetic voice like Jeremiah's are not the same, though the poetic and the prophetic today may often be indistinguishable. However, each may be found by way of a similar process; they may pace different paths, with different rhyme, rhythm and reason, but they each pace; they mark time to a beat that is both deep within and far beyond the pedestrian; they find their stride within very similar processes because 'the following of art is little different from the following of religion in the intense preoccupation it demands'.[10] The responsibility of the poet is to listen in and speak out what they hear – an action that in itself is transformative. Socially and politically poetry can leave it at that. Prophets too must listen-in and speak-out what they hear, but they cannot leave it at that. Therefore, if Yahweh is to speak then prophets, even very young prophets, must be helped to enter their stride, must be encouraged to find a voice. Religious education must nourish the capacity to search-by-ear. It must provide the space within which and the paths along which a wise passiveness, a mesmerised listening-in, finding-a-voice and speaking-out may be practised. Only by entering their stride, by finding their voice within the Judeo-Christian tradition's aural-imaginative pathways can teachers and learners – young or old, male and female, single or married – hope to keep that tradition going today.

Finding a voice means that you can get your own feeling into your own words and that your words have the feel of you about them; and I believe that it may not even be a metaphor, for a poetic voice is probably very intimately connected with the poet's natural voice, the voice that he hears as the ideal speaker of the lines he is making up.[11]

I pause momentarily now, on the path along which my preoccupations have been pacing up and down, to consider Heaney's observation: that voice – to take the physical one for the moment – is not as individual as it might first appear for it is already marked with inherited family traits, intoned with a local accent and carrying with it resonances of a wider national accent, not to mention its being 'grammar-ed' within a shared mother tongue. Therefore the uniqueness of the poetic voice should not be confused with individualism because every poetic voice is imprinted by the literary tradition of which it is a part, even if its part is to kick against tradition. The finding of a religious voice closely parallels the finding of a poetic voice. It too will be related to the uniqueness of the God-given physical voice, passed on orally and accented with familial, local and national tones, cadences, emphases, colour, texture, pace, energies and so on, that make it 'flesh'. It will be imprinted by the religious tradition of which it is a part, and which itself is carried on the breath of the familial, local, national and universal church tradition. And it is because it is carried within these sets of 'vocal chords' that it can check itself out and safeguard itself against individualism or extreme fanaticism.

I get up off the ground now and begin walking again, wondering from the point of view of finding my voice as a religion teacher what resources poetry and its composing process might have to offer. Perhaps finding a voice is not a once-off happening but a life-long learning. Perhaps it is a process that applies not only to the student but is even more urgently a critical process for the teacher who would nourish the process in others today. To speak – as it seems Jesus did – with *authority* in education and in religious education today is not so much to speak with the power or status bestowed by qualifications, or appointed position, but it is to have listened in and attuned one's ear to the voices within the register of the teaching tradition. Within those, to have found one's voice as teacher is to begin to speak authentically, to have been 'authorised'. Like the natural voice, the teacher-voice, despite a culture of increasing standardisation and uniformity in education, will be unique, but its uniqueness will often carry familial intonations, modulations from primary and secondary school experience as well as echoes of the 'teaching tradition' of which it is a part. I cannot find my teacher-voice outside this 'choir'. This choir is a mixture of Greek, Celtic and Judeo-Christian voices; its teacher/singer is a mixture of philosopher, poet and prophet. Coming to know the self as a teacher, finding my religion-teacher voice can therefore only be carried out in a process of mesmerised attention and listening-in to those 'echoes and invitations within' the personal, the local and the traditional – in this case the Judeo-Christian tradition – of which that voice is a part. These voices invite me to listen in to my own experience now, and so as I begin to write about my own experience, my motivation – I hope – is not the product of too much egotism but the response to an injunction to 'know thyself'; in short, to practise what I preach. I seek to model a process of imagining-into-words what I hear of the Judeo-Christian as I listen in to the familial, the local and the traditional within my own experience. I do so in order that I may speak out – again not in the hope of 'success', but in the hope that what I say has meaning. However, the teaching and learning community that I return it to will be the ultimate judge of that.

Exploring experience

In the context of this present work I believe I may have found something of my own voice as a teacher, providentially, by coming across it along the way, much the same as Muirgen came across Fergus's gravestone. It must be said though that the stone I came across as I walked along was more of an irritating stone-in-the-shoe than anything as grandly significant as a gravestone. Having looked at education through the archetypal images of nourishing and leading out towards light or darkness, I had originally planned to continue my journey by exploring the Exodus story. This story offered the possibility of another archetypal image of education as a leading-out, this time from slavery to freedom. It also offered an image of education as a 'nourishing' in the form of the Passover ritual – both its food and its narrative-nourishment. From this position, links to Jesus the Teacher, food, the sharing of bread, injunctions to 'feed lambs and sheep' and so on were fairly obvious and promising. I was reluctant to abandon this plan since in my own mind it provided what I was looking for; it offered 'shelter' that I could comfortably settle into for the duration of this chapter. Ironically I now realise that this shelter was a Greek cave offering refuge from the original anxiety about how or where to go in this chapter. I had not so much *found,* as *forced* an entry into the Judeo-Christian tradition. And in doing so I was ultimately at risk not of finding a voice but of what a former singing teacher had always warned against: 'forcing your voice'. However, the cave offered refuge from the uncertainty, from the 'unknowing', that is critical – that is in a way the pearl of great price – of religious education. It offered a plan, a leading-out towards the light at the end of the tunnel, the seductive promise of a methodological proceeding-without-doubt, to the end of the chapter. How powerful this archetype's influence, even after all I had written!

This plan had certain logic and even though somewhere within myself I worried that it was all a bit predictable, I preferred it to the vague hunch and the persistent muttering in the back of my mind that 'he taught them in *parable*' might be worth listening-in to. In the end though even something as seemingly insignificant as the stone in the shoe had a way of insisting that I stop and address the situation. It was in doing so that I came to realise:

> There is the metaphor that is less a metaphor, because it is the metaphor I choose; there is the metaphor that is more deeply, more irrevocably a metaphor because it chooses me ...[12]

The metaphor or archetypal image of Judeo-Christian education that I believe 'chose me', that worked *against* the grain of my Greek rational impulses, though probably 'with' the Celtic-poetic, presented itself locally.

Experiencing the biblical-in-the-local

I have never strolled the streets of Nazareth nor browsed the market in Capernaum; I have never visited the Temple in Jerusalem nor stood on the banks of the River Jordan; I have never been out in a boat on the Sea of Galilee nor spoken to the people who, for generations, lived on its shores and fished its waters; I have no experience of the actual physicality of biblical places but I have heard of them through biblical stories carried like delicate bubbles on the breath of religious tradition from there-and-then to here-and-now. What I *do* have experience of is the Fair Hill market in Ballymena; I have stood waiting for the school bus in Magherafelt's Broad Street, observing this mid-Ulster town go about its four o'clock business; I have visited the Cathedral in Armagh on solemn-high liturgical occasions; I have lived on the shores of Lough Neagh, among the people of Toomebridge, some of whom still farm its hinterland or still fish eels, salmon, pollan and brown trout in its waters; I have travelled up the River Bann in my father's boat, through the lock gates at Toome and out onto Lough Neagh. Sometimes the lough was calm, sometimes it was 'rough enough'. Up until now, however, the biblical and the local had at best existed side-by-side in my experience. They had never *coincided* in my imagination. The bubbles had never burst. Why they did so now I can only hazard a guess that a call came to 'listen then if you have ears'. I can only suppose that, in sitting down to investigate the stone in my shoe, something in that stone caught my attention and 'mesmerised'. I suspect that both poetry and parable reached into the activity of listening in to the tradition's whisperings in the back of my mind. At any rate something stirred in the meeting in imagination's landscape of biblical and local lakes, an in-rush of blood to the memory, surfacing old associations and sponsoring trances of thought and mountings of the mind.

I remembered those Sunday afternoons when we went out on the lough in my father's boat. Perhaps it was the fact that it was hand-built that made me always nervous, despite the lifejacket, as I took my place among my brothers and sisters. Perhaps it was the swarms of Lough Neagh flies like millions of jitters that sponsored a certain resistance to the intended pleasure of the experience. Perhaps it was the myth that Lough Neagh's waters could turn wood to stone, in which case our boat would sink and we would be eaten by millions of eels. The eel, that 'rib of water drawn/Out of water',[13] was, according to local lore, constituted completely of nerves, which was why, even when they were 'dead' and after they were dead even when they were skinned, and after they were dead and skinned, even when they were chopped up and frying in the pan, they had been known to wriggle and twitch. Their skins had healing properties:

> When a wrist was bound with eelskin, energy
> Redounded in that arm, a waterwheel
> Turned in the shoulder, mill-races poured
> And made your elbow giddy.
> Your hand felt unrestrained and spirited.[14]

Eel fishing is a night-time activity closely related to 'The Dark' and I remember getting up one Sunday morning, going to wash my face before Mass, turning the tap and shrieking at the sight of a sink full of these writhing things and hearing later about those who had been 'out fishing all night and had caught nothing!' I remember that in my child-mind the word 'treacherous' was somehow hyphenated to the word 'lough' and I know from experience remembered the fear felt by those who were in the boat out on the stormy lake. Perhaps they too had heard the saying 'The lough will claim a victim every year'. I remember my fisherman friend, the late John McGuckian and almost laugh out loud as I see him in my imagination, his hand shading his eyes, straining to figure out who is on the shore at this hour of the morning, with a fire lit and 'the pan on'. 'It can't be,' he's saying to himself. 'It couldn't be … could it? Jesus! Maybe … but here? No!' He ties up and comes ashore. 'Bring some fish with you,' the figure calls to him. John turns back to his boat, incredulous, obedient.

In my experience of the coincidence of these two fresh water lakes, Lough Neagh and the Sea of Galilee, it seemed as though ancient and un-nameable energies stirred. Wordsworth in *The Prelude* addressed similar energies in his experience of Lake Derwent as 'Wisdom and Spirit of the Universe!' As I continue walking, I suspect that in the space or vacuum opened up by my hesitation in proceeding according to the pre-planned, i.e. the Exodus, route, something within the wisdom and spirit of the universe occasioned in my mind an in-rush of images and memories around these two lakes. Like a Waves-of-Story words, images, memories and associations from both lakes co-mingled and danced together, weaving and waving, swirling and ceilí swinging, gathering momentum all the time. Caught up in that momentum intellectualisations and intuitions about the significance of these two waters began to gather and grow,

> ... into a new momentum – that all entered me
> like an access of free power, as if belief
> caught up and spun the objects of belief
> in an orbit coterminous with longing.[15]

Like Lough Neagh flies, biblical and local images and stories swarm my memory. Like eels, connections between the biblical and the local begin to wriggle and register 'live' in my imagination. Reeling metaphorically, I reach out of this 'visitation' to steady myself. I find that my hand is once again being taken and I am:

> ... being handed down
> Into a boat that dipped and shilly-shallied
> Scaresomely every time. We sat tight
> On short cross benches, in nervous two's and three's
> Obedient, newly close, nobody speaking
> Except the boatman, as the gunwales sank
> And seemed they might ship water any minute.
> The sea was calm but even so,
> When the engine kicked and our ferryman
> Swayed for balance, reaching for the tiller,
> I panicked at the shiftiness and heft of the craft itself.

> What guaranteed us –
> That quick response and buoyancy and swim –
> Kept me in agony ...[16]

Through this poem it is as though I am being handed down into this boat as it dips and shilly-shallies scaresomely. I find in the experience what I believe to be a point of departure. Having entered the Celtic tradition by way of the swallow hole in the poem 'Undine', I now find myself, through this poem, being handed down into an archetypal image of the Judeo-Christian teaching tradition as 'Teaching from the Boat'. I reach out and take the hand that hands me down ...

My co-travellers in the boat are fellow students of Mount Oliver Institute of Pastoral Education in 1985. We are embarking on an educational 'outing'. We have been handed down into some kind of educational craft built to facilitate something called 'learning through experience' – in this case the experience of being a student of this particular institute of religious education. We sit tight, newly close in small groups, nobody speaking as the ties to the *terra firma*, the solid educational ground and the surefootedness of lectures, tutorials and seminars, are unloosed. Outwardly all is calm but even so ... what guarantees? We begin 'sailing evenly across/The deep, still seeable-down-into water, of our experience' but what about the unfathomable and non-seeable-down-into depths of our experience further out? Nobody speaks and I have the sinking feeling as I avoid all eye contact that this whole enterprise might ship panic-stricken giggles any minute and sink without trace of anything other than bubbles of gurgling laughter. The mounting pressure of our collective silence as we sit there in a group eventually forces the lid I have been keeping on my silence and suddenly some engine kicks to life and as though powered by the memory of a story, a parable told from another boat on another occasion, I find myself on my feet, the very unsteady letter of that same parable that was told on another occasion from another boat:

'Once upon a time ... there was this man who went out to sow seed ... *oops! it doesn't begin 'once upon a time' though ... it's not a 'once upon a time' story ... I sway for balance* ... and he scattered some seed here and he scattered some there ... *and basically some grew and some didn't – how do I make a tellable story out of such an unremarkable plot; I'll have to spin it out a bit* ... And some of the seed fell on this kind of rough stony ground and it didn't do very well because it couldn't get any roots there and the birds spied it and came and ate most of it anyway ... *It's hard to put down roots in this non-story; I sway for balance* ... And he scattered some of the seed on other ground where there wasn't much shelter ... *not much by way of shelter in this story either, it's all out in the open, exposed ... like myself trying to tell it, all at sea really* ... so the sun got at it and scorched it and so it didn't do very well either ... And then he scattered some more seed ... *do I feel a breeze?* ... and it fell on ground that was all thorns and briars and the seed got choked ... so it didn't do very well either ... *is this parable gathering a momentum all of its own? I'll have to fight for control, take longer pauses; speak more slowly, 'bring her round'* ... And some of the seed he scattered managed to land on good ground and ... *It is 'as if I look from another boat/Sailing through air, far up, and can see/How riskily I fare '* ... well it grew, in fact it did really well, so ... *No! Not 'so' wrong word ... you've taken a wrong turn, go back three spaces ... I turn to look for the shore, I want to go back now* ... So the man who had sowed it ... *no! he's long gone he left in the very first line ... You're on your own* ... gathered up the harvest ... *Help! I don't know how to sail this thing* ... and he, ... *but 'he' didn't anything because he's long gone; I've lost it now, the wind and the current of this parable are carrying me further and further out to sea ...* and he brought it all into his store ... *Like the time when as a child I sat on the big stone at the edge of the Lough Neagh ...* and put it all into bags ... *suddenly that stone seemed to be moving, panic, panic ...* and then he brought the bags to the miller ... *I'm on that stone now ...* and the miller turned the grain into flour and ... *it is moving, but rocks don't move and they don't float in water ... neither do parables but that is what's happening ...* the miller brought the flour home and ... *but there's no miller in the original story ... this whole thing is way out at sea, uncontrollable ... it's carrying me with it ...* made lots of loaves of bread and ... *somebody help ...* he kept some of the bread for his family and ... *Help, ...* he sold the rest in the market ... *please, make it stop* ... And with the money he got he bought some more seed and ... *please ...* one day ... *now ...* he went out and started scattering all over again. The end. *The wind dies down, the rock has stopped moving; the boat is returning to the shore, bringing me back, head 'bare and bowed'. Phew!*

Innocently, I believed as I set out in that experience that I was simply telling a fairly unremarkable story, in my own words to a group of fellow students and teachers. But something in the experience of struggling through the actual telling of the parable unnerved me. It was as though I encountered something reminiscent of the 'voluntary power instinct/uprearing its head' that sent the young Wordsworth scuttling home from his boat trip on Lake Derwent[17] with a 'dim and undetermined sense/Of unknown modes of being'. Similarly, in the act of telling this parable of the Sower, something in the uncontrollable twists and turns of a story I supposed to be easy and innocent reared its head, raised its voice, revealed a power, a depth charge that was live, current, electric. I found myself improvising and crossing plot-paths with other half-remembered fairy stories from my childhood. And all the time, tricky currents within the experience of telling threatened to sink the whole risky enterprise.[18] Something unnerving in the experience of telling that parable on that occasion sent *me* scuttling homeward too, with an equally dim and undetermined sense of unknown modes of being in the deep waters of this Jewish teacher's parable-tradition. Working from a vantage point of some twenty years later, I sense that the linguistic lake in which parable lives has its own share of narrative eels that twitch and wriggle still, long after they have been 'landed', skinned, chopped up, fried and served in bite-size interpretations. It seems that you may catch a parable but, as I discovered in the telling, that does not mean you can hold onto it – even two thousand years later.

Like all of his parables, this parable told by Jesus from a boat on the Sea of Galilee has hidden currents and eddies. Despite their surface appearance, under the surface they are as dangerous as they are dynamic, as potent as they are nonchalant. The shilly-shallying uncertainty and uncontrollable motions and fluencies of water are an image of the very currents the everyday experience they deal with is composed of. At the heart of parable's dealings with the everyday reality is the daunting question 'What guarantees?' Language is the boat by which religious education engages these currents and questions and uncertainties. For Jesus the boat in whose shiftiness and heft, in whose buoyancy and swim, he trusted was a Jewish craft–parable. Parable is the boat down into which he hands his listeners so that they may experience life's shiftiness and heft and yet trust it to word's buoyancy and swim. As John Dominic Crossan says, Jesus' parables seek 'to assist people to find their own ultimate encounter ... to help them into their own experience of the kingdom and to draw from that experience their own way of life'.[19] To come close to parable's way with language is to come close to their teller, their teaching and ultimately their teacher and his God:

> The fact that Jesus' experience is articulated in metaphorical parables, and not in some other linguistic types, means that these expressions are part of that experience itself ... There is an intrinsic and inalienable bond between Jesus' experience and Jesus' parables. A sensitivity to the metaphorical language of religious and poetic experience and an empathy with the profound and mysterious linkage of such experience and such expression may help us to understand what is most important about Jesus: his experience of God.[20]

For the religion teacher, the Jewish and Judeo-Christian influence of parable and a sensitivity to the poetic provide 'the absolute register to which your pedagogic ear has to be tuned'.[21] An approach to parable must be made via imagination, particularly the audial imagination, because to work with parable is to play it by ear; it is to pay mesmerised attention, maintain a wise passiveness, to 'ponder in the heart'; it is not so much hear, as to 'sense [the presence and action of God], through hearing'.

To set out in search of the essential quick of the Judeo-Christian teacher voice within myself and the religious educational tradition within which I have grown up, and to end up in the presence of this parable of the Sower, taught from the boat, may not be all that surprising. It was on this particular occasion that Jesus' response to the need of the crowd then (as now) was to relocate himself, to push the boundaries, to 'put himself out' in order to be more clearly audible.[22] On this occasion Jesus turned up the sound as he drew this slippery rib of language up out of the Jewish underworld, out of the 'glooms and whorls and slatings'[23] of the Jewish prophetic tradition. That prophetic tradition's imagination was his 'Ground of being', the site of his 'Body's deep obedience/To all its shifting tenses'. In terms of

Jesus the Teacher, that deep obedience, or obedience-to-the-deep and to its shifting tenses, is imaged in this instance in his teaching from the boat. In pushing out from the shore, in teaching from the boat, what Jesus turns the sound up on, I suggest, is the voice of that *oral tradition*, of the God of the Old Testament whose spirit 'hovered over the waters', who breathed, who spoke, who drew a rib of live narrative out of silent Creation and entered it into conversation with humanity. It is the tradition of the God who, in Jesus, adds a unique parabolic note to the Jewish narrative register.[24] Crossan has said, 'Parable is always a somewhat unnerving experience'.[25] My experience of parable suggests to me that this may be so because the parables of Jesus are wriggling eels, composed or 'constituted' out of nerve; sheer linguistic nerve. As a genre they form the central nervous system of the Kingdom or Reign of God; they are biblical narrative 'skinned' and still twitching; they are the nerve of the Word of God, then and now – live. Encounter parable and you touch that nerve. Shocking!

Much has been written on parable but what is of most interest to me is not interpretations of what the parables say because 'what is most strikingly absent in the original syntactics of Jesus' parables is precisely this clear terminal application and explanation'.[26] In other words, 'he who finds the meaning loses it, he who loses it finds it'.[27] And besides, what T.S. Eliot has said of poetry rings true, for me, for parable also: 'it is never what a poem *says* that matters, but what it is.'[28] Parable is an experience or it is not heard, and it is heard via the audial imagination if it is heard at all. It is the audial imagination that, as I quoted elsewhere, operates far below conscious levels of thought and feeling, returning to an origin and bringing something back. To experience parable in this way is to be impossibly 'at sea' on a moving rock. Like the panic-stricken child we as adults may protest that this cannot be happening, that this is not possible, but it continues to happen even as we sit unbelievably through it. To encounter parable is to have 'put into question' our own faculties – for instance, reason, will, the senses – by which we measure reality; it is to experience in the present the subversion in language of all one has previously taken to be the 'fixed' nature of reality. It is to be in agony, facing the question that only tends to receive recognition in dire or in searching postmodern circumstances: 'What guarantees us?' Religious education must foster the asking of this very question because in the asking there is already a critical admission, or confession, of uncontrollability, lack of power over life, lack of sovereignty over language, lack of control over genuine educational and religious educational 'yield'. Religious education must foster through poetic practice the growth of audial imagination so that Jesus' parables may be heard, so that kingdom – the presence of God among us – continues to come in a world of unanchored change and rapidly shifting certainties.

'It would be strange if Jesus had chosen the parable as his special genre and never reflected on the implications of that choice. This metaparable is the result of that reflection.'[29] It is Jesus teaching about the kingdom and reflecting on how he teaches *as* he teaches. But again it is not what the parable *says* about our primordial, mysterious relationship with the earth; about human 'going out', striving in search of fulfilment; about the way in which methods and reasons for failure tend to be spelled out while the precise modes of success tend not to be detailed in any way; about the God-given gift of yield; about how the kingdom is unlikely to arrive overwhelmingly, like a fan-fared Queen of Sheba, but by way of the normal and natural processes of losses and gains – it is not any of these which are primary, it seems to me. Behind or below these is parable's etymological root system – seed, semen, semantic; the intercourse of Word and Kingdom. This parable, as all parables, riddles the relationship between the nature of Jesus' language and the kingdom of Jesus' God. It is on the surface tension of this linguistic relationship that religious education must push out from the shore and teach from the boat, setting a course that navigates from moment to moment, from motion to motion, life's shiftiness and heft, and language's buoyancy and swim. All the while it must plumb the depths of the agonising and tantalising question at the heart of experience: 'What guarantees?'

Having said earlier that the kind of knowledge involved in coming to know the Judeo-Christian tradition, the possible presence of the Risen Teacher at work in oneself and one's educational environs today, is primarily a work of imagination and that that work is carried out in *words*, what I have tried to imagine into words here is a – modest – example of the kind of coming to know that I have been talking about. What I have found in the pocket of the Judeo-Christian tradition is (another kind of egg really) a seed. Having gone in search of the presence of the Judeo-Christian and the Risen Teacher; having engaged with the signs and symbols, the lore and narrative in personal, local and biblical landscape along the way; and, through them, having been drawn beyond the ground of my usual, reasonable surefootedness, I found myself ultimately at sea in the presence of the parable[30] of the Sower. But it was poetry that brought me there; poetry has been the ferryman; it was poetry that attuned my ear to the 'essential quick'[31] of this Judeo-Christian voice and offered critical resources for a deeper understanding of the experience. It was poetry and one institution's imaginative approach to religious education that together offered the telling opportunity in which my own voice could vibrate off this particular teaching parable. While Wordsworth and Jeremiah paced the paths of their various traditions finding their voice and entering their stride as poet and prophet, entering one's stride and finding one's voice as Judeo-Christian religion teacher requires the navigation of parable's plot-paths, which in this case offer not so much 'crunch and scuffle' as shilly-shally underfoot. To teach from the boat is to take the original Teacher's lead, to take risks similar to those he took in quitting the firm ground of the 'guiding plot decisions of his own tradition' so that his stories went out on their own. It is to leave the well-worn educational plot-paths of the modern-methodological and, at least now and again, to risk 'A farewell to surefootedness', putting faith in what lies 'a pitch/Beyond our usual hold upon ourselves'.[32] To teach from the boat is to find myself handed down into a process and a tradition in which, as a teacher, I must learn to live and cope with feelings of panic as I sway for balance amidst the urges of Church and society today for guarantees – proven socio-economic or religious yields – and the scaresome risk and shilly-shally of a primary education intimate with the poetic and prophetic.

However, it is worth pointing out that it was Jesus – not the crowd – who pushed out from the shore. Therefore it seems to me that it is the teacher, not her pupils, that has to take that risk. In doing so she allows the possibility of encountering what allows her to find her voice and amplify it, speak with first-hand authority rather than second-hand knowledge. To teach from the boat is pedagogically to place oneself positively at the mercy of 'what guarantees' which is the question central to the parable of the Sower, to education and to life itself. To teach from the boat is to place oneself at pedagogic risk in a new and scaresome relation to educational reality. The religious educator cannot make a preferential option for imagination; imagination is not a value-added decoration. Religious education is powered by imagination or else it is neither educational nor religious. To teach from the boat is to wrap parabolic eel-skins around the religious–educational imagination of both the teacher and pupil so that 'energy redounds in its arms, a waterwheel turns in its shoulder, mill-races pour and make its elbow giddy and its hand feel unconstrained and spirited'.[33] By virtue of such spirited energies religious education may be an experience, an expression of 'kingdom coming'.

Notes

1. *Primary School Curriculum; Introduction:* 'It is the responsibility of the school to provide a religious education consonant with its ethos and at the same time to be flexible in making alternative organisational arrangements for those who do not wish to avail of the particular religious education it offers … the Education Act (1998), recognises the rights of the different church authorities to design curricula in religious education at primary level and to supervise their teaching and implementation, a religious education curriculum is not included in these curriculum documents.' Dublin, The Stationery Office, 1999, p. 58.

2. Heaney, *Finders Keepers: Selected Prose 1971–2001*, London, Faber and Faber, 2002, p. 47.

3. *Real Presences*, The University of Chicago Press, 1989, p. 3.

4. Heaney, *The Redress of Poetry: Oxford Lectures*, London, Boston, Faber and Faber, 1995, p. xiv.

5. From the very start this brings Theology – up until now, religious education's reference point – into intimate association with the poetic. It is an intimacy of the kind courted since the sixties by such as Robert Funk:
   'The study of theology ought to begin these days with a study of poetry. This is not merely to hand a rose to the poets, but to advocate a sane programme of theological rehabilitation, certainly of theological repatriation. Theology seems to have … wandered so far afield that it has forgotten the wellsprings of its infancy. The antidote must be potent enough to restore sight to the blind and hearing to the deaf. Perhaps modern poetry is sufficiently strong medicine …' The operative word being 'perhaps'. See *The New Orpheus*, op. cit., p. 88.

6. In this regard, discussions in relation to the paternalistic authority of Theology versus the oedipal challenge to that

authority from Religious Education have little chance of maturing unless *both* are prepared to *confess* – in a positive sense – their need for intimacy with and their dependency on the poetic.

7. *Preoccupations*, p. 63.
8. Ibid., p. 65.
9. Ibid., p. 68.
10. Yeats, W.B., 'Samhain: 1905' in *Explorations,* cited by Heaney in *Preoccupations*.
11. Ibid., p. 43.
12. Rago, H., in *The Poet in His Poem,* Bulletin of the Midwest Modern Language Association, Vol. 2, *Poetic Theory/Poetic Practice*, 1969, pp. 52–8.
13. From Heaney, *Seeing Things*, London, Faber and Faber, 1991, p. 73.
14. Ibid.
15. Heaney, 'Wheels within Wheels' from *Seeing Things*, op. cit., p. 46.
16. Ibid., p. 16.
17. *The Prelude*, 1799, 1805, 1850, New York, London, W.W. Norton and Company, 1979, 'The Two-Part Prelude of 1799', p. 3.
18. The experience of telling the story hints at what Crossan describes in relation to the plot-paths of another parable, concerning the finding of a pearl of great price: 'At this point Jesus' story has departed the guiding plot decisions of his own tradition and the story is on its own.' *Finding Is The First Act: Trove Folktales and Jesus' Treasure Parable*, Philadelphia, Fortress Press; Missoula, Montana, Pennsylvania Scholars Press, 1979, p. 89.
19. *In Parables: The Challenge of the Historical Jesus*, Sonoma, California, Polebridge Press, 1992, p. 51.
20. Ibid., p. 22.
21. *Preoccupations*, p. 44.
22. It is interesting that in regard to his parables and their teaching Crossan locates the official teachers of Jesus' day and their teaching: '(1) within a group authority; (2) within an official synagogue; (3) within a 'canonical' text. Jesus on the other hand, taught: (1) outside this group authority; (2) outside the synagogue by the lakeside [indeed on this occasion, *on* the lake]; (3) outside the 'canonical' texts.' *Cliffs of Fall: Paradox and*

Polyvalence in the Parables of Jesus, New York, The Seabury Press, 1980, pp. 16–17.

23. *Seeing Things*, p. 73.
24. '... the creative and poetic narrative parable was a pedagogical genre almost totally undeveloped by the early Church itself and which does not seem to have been prevalent in Jewish tradition until somewhat later.' *Cliffs of Fall*, p. 49.
25. *The Dark Interval: Towards a Theology of Story*, Illinois 60648, Argus Communications Niles, 1975, p. 56.
26. *Cliffs of Fall*, p. 19.
27. Eliot, T.S., *The Use of Poetry and the Use of Criticism*, Faber paper covered edition, 1933, p. 17.
28. Ibid., p. 18.
29. *Cliffs of Fall*, p. 50.
30. ' ... The Sower seems somewhat different from many of Jesus' other parables. I would maintain ... that this difference arises from the fact that it is not just a teaching about the Kingdom, although it is that as well, but also a teaching about teaching about the Kingdom. It is not just a parable about the Kingdom, although it is that as well, but rather as a metaparable, it is a parable about parables of the Kingdom. As such it tells us about the parabler himself, about the parabled Kingdom and about the very parable itself as well.' *Cliffs of Fall*, p. 49.
31. *Preoccupations*, p. 44.
32. *Seeing Things*, p. 86.
33. Ibid., p. 73

4 Making an Entrance

With poetry as a guide through the first three chapters of this book I have sought to understand something of the nature of teaching and learning by exploring archetypal images of education. Digging up its past, I have sought to 'divine' dynamic energies lurking deep within educational tradition, revealing how those energies still course through, or are staunched in, education's present – even if for the most part sub-consciously. But at this point the omnipresent bell is ringing, bringing my deliberations to a close – for now. It is time to scrape the crusts and wrappings of my thoughts and imaginings into the bin, stuff other unfinished ramifications and associations into my lunch-box where they may offer nourishment for another day, snap the lid shut, deposit my mug among those already in the sink, and head back into the *real-practik* of the classroom. I make my way along the corridor-of-transition from the adult company of my colleagues – Plato, Homer, the Nurse, Senchán, Heaney, Jesus the Parabler etc. – to that of my pupils. As I enter the classroom and call things to a more practical order, I remember that it was in fact the practical work of the classroom, the active engagement with children, poetry and its writing process that led me to or sponsored those musings in the first half of this book *and not the other way around*. Through this process the conviction that 'poetry is the deepest education there is' has been confirmed. Critically though, poetry as an educational role model will not tolerate for long the separation of practice and reflection-on-practice. So without further ado:

Where Does Poetry Come From?
It's stuck to my jumper like fluff
Poetry is plucky sorta' stuff.
It's stuck like a tat in my hair
However it got tangled up there.
It's stuck to my fingers like jam
And I'm lickin' it still so I am.
It's stuck like a fly in my eye
And made it water and cry.
It's stuck on my knee like the grime
Of the plaster's left-over black line.
It's stuck on my tongue like a hair
That came from – I don't know where.
Where does poetry come from?
(3rd/4th class; P.5/6)

I'm fond of his poem because it was a *relief*. It was the first attempt by myself and this third/fourth class at writing together. It is *our* poem. It was a relief that, having decided to 'give poetry a go', having opened the door and invited it into our classroom so to speak, a poem actually 'turned up'. It was a relief to know that poetry and poetry writing does not have to come from some exotic location outside ourselves, but resides, at least some of the time, very close by the completely ordinary and intimately known. It was a relief to know that we could 'home-make' something that looked and sounded like a poem, that had pattern and form and shape, that could 'speak up for itself' and that we could recognise as authentic. And I am fond of it because, as a teacher, I was genuinely surprised by it, and very pleasantly so. I remember smiling bemusedly at it on the blackboard and feeling that impulsive confidence Heaney mentions, the confidence that gives rise to a sense that 'perhaps we could do this poetry thing too'.[1] But what I am fondest of in this poem is the mixture of craft and gift that it reflects. It is true to say that the poem 'turned up', was a gift, beginner's luck and all that. But it is also true that we had to find a way to put shape on the luck, or as Yeats said, to bring it within the jurisdiction of form. Even in this initial engagement with poetry we learned from experience that poetry is made out of a mixture of craft and gift.

> Learning the craft is learning to turn the windlass at the well of poetry. Usually you begin by dropping the bucket half-way down the shaft and winding up a taking of air. You are miming the real thing until one day the chain draws unexpectedly tight and you have dipped into waters that will continue to entice you back. You'll have broken the skin on the pool of yourself.[2]

The children and teacher making this poem have been lucky to break the skin on the pool that is ourselves-in-writing. We are having a go at raising poetry and its writing process like a bucket of water from the well of our everyday experience, to haul it up and pour it into the classroom container. And although we are learning the job of how to craft lines in order to create a structure to 'carry' the poem, we do not – cannot – know in advance of writing this poem what sort of structure will be needed or how the poem will turn out; the learning and the doing are inseparable:

> ... in genuine artistic endeavor there can never be a way of putting together what is to be expressed in advance of expressing it.[3]

We learn by going where we have to go. Primary education that models itself on poetry's artistry endorses a way-of-knowing that is not predictable, a 'knowing' that is inseparable from 'doing'. It recognises the limits of our power-of-intention so that we cannot pre-plan or pre-script poetry writing lessons with predictable, intended learning outcomes. While we may narrate in retrospect the story of how the poem came to be, we could not predict it in advance. This puts the essence of poetry and its writing process beyond methodological control.

The practice of poetry writing is about a process, not just about a product, a view endorsed by the 1999 curriculum, 'Writing is primarily an expressive process'. 'Where Does Poetry Come From?' is a response through a writing process, to the pupils' and teachers' experience of being, like many of their peers, 'in-the-dark' with regard to the 'whole story' about poetry. Many of them, up until now, had only ever seen a poem in its ideal, i.e. its finished form, as Bullock says, 'something more or less involuntarily secreted by the author'.[4] For them poetry always arrived fully formed on the page, sprung like Athena from the head of Zeus, full-born out of some poet's brain. Exactly where it came from and how it was made was a mystery they had not even thought about. 'Where Does Poetry Come From?' is what Heaney might call a literal 'feeling into words';[5] in a very physical sense a 'feel for poetry'. It gropes, pokes, licks, rubs and fingers words and images from the children's experience of their own bodies and arranges their 'findings' in the bodily structure of a poem; six rhyming couplets and a question. The process of writing the poem leads its participants in a kind of dance; an advance-and-retire movement in which moments of intimate disclosure, of coming face to face with a classicist particularity and detail – the tat in the hair, the fly in the eye, the hair on the tongue – are in a continuous dialectic with the more romantic mystery of 'however they got there'; in other words, the definitive in the context of the indefinable, or is it the other way around! It is a children's game of hide-and-seek, a playful happening-in-language, a game of words between poetry's writing process and its writers. It is an attempt to pin poetry down, to 'make it stick' as something that is real enough to stimulate a response – licking one's fingers, making one's eyes water and so on. It brings poetry well within the current of normal physical life. It is an example of the way in which art is an activity engaged in

> ... deliberately and responsibly by people who know what they are doing, even though they do not know in advance what is going to come of it.[6]

Education itself is often an activity engaged in deliberately and responsibly by people who know what they are doing even if they do not know in advance what is going to come of a particular lesson or indeed of a particular *lifetime* in education. The children and teacher engaged in crafting this poem know what they are doing – they are searching: searching their experience, literally searching themselves, 'body and bones'. They are searching for something – even if they are not sure what exactly. Although the pupils do not know it by these words, what they are doing is searching for what T.S. Eliot might have called 'objective correlatives', which can act as concrete realisations of the nature of poetry. They are searching for what the imagination of Jesus the Parabler searched for in an attempt to find metaphors for the Kingdom or Reign of God. The metaphors he 'turned up' were not just descriptions of that reality but *actual expressions of it*.

And though the pupils do not know *exactly* what it is they are looking for, neither are they completely ignorant because they know from their everyday experience of searches such as that detailed below that hidden things often have an elusive 'whatever, wherever, whenever' quality about them. This usually means that if you search hard enough (though there is no guarantee), 'something will turn up', which is exactly what happens. After what Bullock might have called 'a search for techniques appropriate to [the poets'] intention',[7] the poem 'turns up'.

> **Lost**
> Even if they're found again
> They'll soon be lost again
> The keys of the car
> Mammy's purse
> The baby's bottle
> The remote control
> The scissors and sellotape
> The yoke for whatever
>
> **And found**
> Down the back of the sofa
> Under the telly
> In Daddy's trouser's pocket
> Out in the car
> In the jam-jar behind the curtain on the kitchen window
> In the bottom of my schoolbag
> Or my swimming bag
> Where you left it.
> (3rd/4th class; P.4/5)

In the beginning what is required is faith, like Muirgen, faith-in-searching. In the end the poem is a 'blessing in return'. The faith-statement (that 'something will turn up') is common parlance in everyday life; applied to poetry it is equally a profession of faith in the writing process which can lead pupils and teachers to the same trust Heaney discovered in the process of writing *The Redress of Poetry*, i.e.

> ... the trust ... that a reliable critical course could be plotted by following a poetic sixth sense.[8]

To this statement I would add that a reliable critical educational course may also be plotted by following a poetic sixth sense as much as by following an objective, rational lesson plan. It is the poetic sixth sense that urges one's teaching at times to push out from the shore, to teach from the boat.

At a specifically educational level, the game of hide-and-seek that is being played in this poem or the advance/retire movement of its dance reflects the process whereby a child comes into language in the first place:

> ... by a kind of natural expansion and assimilation, with no conscious master plan, but with new words miraculously finding their place in relation to 'old' ones ... it is of the nature of experience itself that it seeks and finds words that express it.[9]

This seeking and finding is at the heart of *experience* as it is at the heart of genuine primary education. It may be facilitated by methodology but is ultimately a linguistic engagement that takes it beyond methodology because

> ... searching hard, as we often have to do, for just the right word or words to say what needs to be said ... occurs *within* words ... Neither the world of our experience [including religious experience] and understanding, nor our language are available to us independently of each other; they belong together in an indissoluble unity.[10]

Like an itch seeking a scratch, the hide-and-seek format of this poem and its writing process is an example of poetry as a game in which experience seeks language and language seeks experience with a view to understanding and living life more fully. Furthermore it seeks an understanding that includes within it an appreciation of life's (often silent) mystery. That mystery is part of the open-ended question that brings this poem to the paradoxical conclusion-that is-a-question. Where does poetry come from? No endeavour is more wholly educational than that which is exemplified in this poem and its writing process. Primarily, education is at its most fully alive when a poetic sixth sense urges one's teaching to push out from the shore, one's experience crafts a boat and one teaches and learns, balanced precariously on the very fluid surface-tension of language and life.

Swimming In Poetry
Can you jump into a poem
Like you jump into a pool
Or do you sit on the edge
And dabble your words
A toe or two at a time?

In the poem 'Where Does Poetry Come From?' the teacher and pupils in a sense took the first option in 'Swimming in Poetry' and just leaped right in. But despite what I have written retrospectively about that poem, it was not any prior knowledge or application of methodology that made it significant. It was an important piece of writing because it verified experientially that 'in practice, you proceed by your own experience of what it is to write what you consider a successful poem. You survive in your own esteem not by the corroboration of theory but by the trust in certain moments of satisfaction which you know intuitively to be moments of extension'.[11] This poem was a gift. But in truth also, one swallow doesn't make a summer and one has to enter and re-enter poetry's pool again and again, dabbling 'A toe or two at a time'. The Cox Report into the teaching of English offers another way in, suggesting that:

> Good primary teachers pay attention to the process of writing developed from knowledge and understanding of the practice of experienced writers (including themselves). They are then able to provide classroom activities which allow children to behave like real writers.[12]

This statement has much to offer that is worth considering with regard to writing but it nevertheless jumps the gun a little. It describes a situation in which the process is already up and running, where the teacher is already familiar with experienced writers and is probably already a practicing writer. To take this statement as one's starting point would be to miss out on how the teacher (who is *critical* in the process) may come to make an entrance into the writing process *herself*. For the teacher, 'making an entrance' is a process in itself. It is a vital piece of experience out of which to find a way for her pupils, especially reluctant ones, to do the same. Teachers who find that poetry is 'outside the current of their life', and perhaps outside the current of their classroom life, (and in this it may have much in common with religion) must find a way to 're-enter the swim' and negotiate poetry's currents as they flow through 'normal life', plumbing the depths of experience as they do so. How teachers may be helped to 'make an entrance' into the poetic swim of things is hinted at in the poem 'Swimming into Poetry'.

I consider myself an example of a teacher/writer who – apart from that first 'mad splash' – sat very reluctantly on the edge of the pool, reluctant even to dabble. I considered myself one of those teachers for whom poetry was most definitely outside the current of my own life and at the very edge of normal classroom life. Nevertheless I propose to give account of my own experience of reluctantly 'entering the swim' for two reasons. Firstly, to offer an insight into the way in which working with poetry draws even those who are reluctant deeper into experience and language. Secondly, to support the belief that working with experience in writing develops one's own language skills and strengthens one's trust in language's creative processes. This trust in language – its buoyancy and swim – is at the heart of anything that would call itself *primary education*. My own experience is of course personal and particular but much of it can, I hope, be harvested-in-language and become educational resource for the lives and learning of other teachers. And so it is to working with my own experience in language that I return once again.

I have recounted in the introduction to this work the story of my own introduction to poetry as part of a post-graduate course of study. The most significant learning for me in remembering and writing that experience was an awareness of a certain poetic prejudice. This prejudice inclined me to the view that poetry was a kind of fancy confectionery, the kind of thing you would not make at home, something 'bought in'. Prejudices are often considered negatively as non-rational, entirely subjective idiosyncrasies that frustrate the achievement of clear, objective analysis and uncompromised understanding of a subject. But without prejudices we would have nothing to think with. Prejudices are the nets with which we fish our experience. To be sure they may be narrow-minded, or they may be very loosely woven and of course it is to be recommended that we try to haul them out of the waters and 'see to them' every so often. But we cannot fish our experience without them. The prejudice that had just come 'fresh' out of the depths of my unconscious as I sat in that group on the first night of the poetry course was critical not just to my understanding of how I viewed poetry but it facilitated a reflective process of understanding-how-I-come-to-understand in the first place. This is a process critical to teaching and learning. Thus that vague hunch that stirred in me that night fostered a hermeneutical perspective, 'a concern to understand the nature and conditions of understanding itself.'[13] That stirring was an example of imaginative activity as an active paying-attention to voices, hunches, instincts, memories and so on, so as to stabilise its state of flux, to distil it into certain words in a certain order.

To use your imagination is – at some level – to pay attention. The question is what kind of attention and to what or whom does one pay. Like the parable in Matthew 13:47-9, it is a sifting of one's catch of vague hunches and gut feelings, pre-understandings and other such instincts and intuitions. This is a process very similar to that which Heaney describes when he speaks of poetry writing:

> *The crucial action is pre-verbal*, to be able to allow the first alertness or come-hither, sensed in a blurred or incomplete way, to dilate and approach as a thought or a theme or a phrase.[14] (my italics)

Or, I would add as a prejudice or hunch. Paying attention by probing these prejudices and impressions in writing, infusing them through the formal ploys of several written drafts with other 'impressions and memories' led me to another level of understanding-how-I-understand-poetry. I knew courtesy of this prejudice my imagination had caught in its net, that I viewed poetry as a 'foreign affair'. I could never engage pupils with something that had never really engaged me, something that was essentially 'beyond' me. I began to speculate about whether or not there was a kind of 'home-made' poetry, and if so what would it look, feel, sound like. This, it 'dawned' on me, lay in my earliest aural memory of the very word 'poetry', an experience of 'name negotiation', as Heaney calls it.[15]

The first time I heard the word 'poetry' it slipped off my teacher's tongue like a dropped stitch from one of her knitting needles. I wasn't quite sure whether she had said 'poetry' or 'poertry'. Being in P.2 at the time, I considered myself a school veteran. I had plotted and plumbed the socio-educational coordinates of the classroom; events like milk-time or lunch-time, giving out things or collecting them or asking to go out to the toilet were all easy and familiar. In fact my only frustration was with the fat-leaded infant's pencil which I reckoned had about as much finesse as a thick lip and which slabbered letters onto my page where they lolled like robotic limbs. But 'poetry', or 'poertry', I had not heard of before. This word was something new and I was curious. In its strange newness I sensed the 'big-noise' clop of something that wore high-heels, a proper school subject with a capital 'P' such as older brothers and sisters in secondary school did. I ran my tongue over its contours, exploring it like the ridges and edges of an emerging tooth. 'Poetry' had an eloquent, sophisticated feel about it. It suggested a cultured, mannerly event, a china-cup-and-saucer. It had the smooth, soft-vowelled texture of sifted flour or sodabread. 'Poertry' on the other hand, with its harshly consonanted 'r', suggested a more down-to-earth business, a rough-hewn affair, a mug, a wheaten farl, a sharpening stone.

Whether a mature or very immature student, the verbal music of home-made poetry was, as Heaney says, 'bedded in the ear' and sucked through the taste buds of the tongue. It resided in such common place as the formal ritual litany of the daily school roll-call; the solemn dignified tones of the signing of the cross; the elastication of one's name across the skin-tight light of the stretch in a spring evening as one was called in for bed; skipping rhymes whose metre was rendered visible in the turning of a rope, like a revolving door repeating its seductive invitation 'in'; the tap dance of feet on hop-scotched paving slabs as one danced across numbered stanzas, negotiating a precarious boundary between classic balance and romantic reach; the alla balla, alla balla of a bouncing ball, like an orbic disembodied pulse; the strict metric rule for counting one's playmates 'in' or 'out'; the pat-pat of a spade on an upturned bucket of sand accompanied by the appeasing incantation to the gods of creativity, 'Castle, castle come out – and I'll give you a penny tomorrow'; the hands-on experience of creating unity of form in one perfect sandcastle among many failures; the lined equidistance of running-a-pole and walking-a-pole on one's way home from school, like pacing oneself over lines of poetry as opposed to paragraphs of prose and so on. The tidal drones cadences and rhythms of many of these rhymes or pre-songs were an inhaling and exhaling of a raw, crude, poetic praxis, a fusion in rhythm of word and action carried on the breath of local oral tradition.

This then is not just a narration of something I had always known but had never thought about or put words on. Without *this expression* in *these words,* I could not know or begin to understand poetry, or my 'self', in the *particular* way I had come to because true creative writing:

> ... is never a repetition or a rehearsal but always in itself a real actualisation both of new meaning and of the person himself in a new way ...[16]

In and through the *expression* of this account I was, unknown to myself, modeling the knowledge-formulating process Bullock describes of bringing knowledge into being through the formulating process of which language is the ordinary means.

And contrary to popular misunderstanding, language at its most 'creative' (and I would add at its most religious) seeks *not* to be generalised, or vague, but to be precise and accurate, so that although the pupils' or teacher's or poet's attempt to bring knowledge into being frequently results in an imprecise mayhem of impressions,

> Now and then I seem to strike a line which is true and clear. The prayer for grace is a prayer for precision. If sin is 'wide of the mark' and imprecise, the state of grace is being precise.[17]

In striving for precision and accuracy, education that engages intimately with language and with the process of poetry writing is already striving to bring experience to its most particular and therefore to its deepest and fullest understanding.

Writing as it has been practiced here has been a learning experience that has nourished this teacher. At the same time it has provided her with an experience that may be harvested as resource for the learning of the students, equipped her with another pocket for them to search. Explicitly, it teaches that

> ... experience is not wordless to begin with and then an object of reflection by being named. ... Rather, it is of the nature of experience itself that it seeks and finds words that express it.[18]

Neither is religious experience wordless to begin with and then an object of reflection by being named. It is of the nature of religious experience too that it seeks and finds words that express it. Seeking and finding and even finding without seeking, as in the parable of the pearl of great price, is the game imagination plays. To 'use your imagination' is to join in this game knowing that you may use all the skills and experience at your disposal to play the game, but you will not be in control of it. At its liveliest, education seeks to create opportunities through which we may both play and explore our experience of playing imagination's game. The role of the poetic in creating such opportunities is vital. What I was learning through writing the piece above was to watch myself learning in much the same way as 'what a student learns in art-school is to watch himself painting'.[19] The kind of knowledge and understanding I as primary teacher gain through this kind of activity cannot be made

> ... accessible through general propositions or guaranteed by intellectual powers alone, ... It cannot be so because it is a knowledge that is particular to the individual's uniqueness, a uniqueness much lauded in primary and indeed education generally, but the inner struggle to create it is less understood. This kind of writing process has to be at the heart of a curriculum that seeks to practically nourish the individual ... knowledge that depends rather on the kind of person one is and is not one without an inner struggle, is not the kind of knowledge that receives recognition in a technocratic culture.[20]

Hopefully similar experience of 'expression' in which they would come to know the subject of their writings, the writing process, and their 'selves', would ring true for my students too. Hopefully too, it is clear from what I have written that a primary education which models itself according to poetry's writing process is less concerned with teaching and learning as programmed and planned activity but hones its skills and practices the better to 'play it [i.e. education] by ear'.

Notes

1. *Preoccupations*, p. 42.
2. Ibid., p. 46.
3. *Back to the Rough Ground*, p. 116.
4. Our recommendations for the National Curriculum emphasises the importance of the writing process as well as the finished product. Primary School Curriculum, op. cit.
5. *Preoccupations*, p. 41.
6. *Back to the Rough Ground*, p. 60.
7. *A Language for Life*, Chap. 11.5, p. 164.
8. *The Redress of Poetry*, London, Faber, 1995, p. xiii.
9. *Back to the Rough Ground*, pp. 143–4.
10. Ibid., p. 138.
11. *Preoccupations*, pp. 54.
12. The Cox Report, *English for Ages 5–11*, Department of Education and Science and the Welsh Office, 1998, Chap. 2:11.
13. *Back to the Rough Ground*, p. 123.
14. *Preoccupations*, pp. 47–9.
15. *An Open Letter*, Field Day Theatre Company, 1983.
16. *Back to the Rough Ground*, p. 68.
17. Brendan Kennelly in *Dark Fathers Into Light*, Bloodaxe Books, 1994, p. 176.
18. *Back to the Rough Ground*, p. 143.
19. Ibid., p. 74.
20. Ibid., p. 75.

5 Attuning the Ear

> Children in primary school playgrounds clearly demonstrate an instinctive pleasure in rhythm, pattern and rhyme. But this will need constant nurturing if it is to develop into an appreciation of the richness of poetry, where words are alive with a plurality of meanings from their contexts, associations and their sensory qualities.[1]

The narrative recounted earlier, instancing the link between language bedding itself in my childhood ear through play and games, hints at two things. Firstly it hints at the inherent playfulness of language (which shall become the focus of attention later). Secondly it points towards what is a micro-part of a larger element in the writing process, something Heaney calls 'attuning the ear'. This is a practice that engages the ear and the voice in 'sounding-out' that instinctive pleasure in rhythm, pattern and rhyme that Cox refers to. In doing so, it promotes the development of 'an ear for language'.[2] To have an ear for language is to be sensitised by 'an aural intelligence' or imagination. It is this auditory imagination that allows one to plumb language's sonic depths and the feeling of syllable and rhythm far below conscious levels of thought and feeling as explored in chapter two. Plumbing language and plumbing the depths of experience are overlapping processes, both intimately educational.

Through the sound dimension of activities such as performance, recitation, learning-by-heart, children continuously repeat the process presented in the following poem:

> ... [lining] up
> Eager to re-enter the long slide
> We were bringing to perfection, time after time
>
> Running and readying and letting go
> Into a sheerness that was its own reward:
> A farewell to surefootedness, a pitch
>
> Beyond our usual hold upon ourselves.
> And what went on kept on going, from grip to give ...[3]

Except that it is not ice they slide along, but the *sound* of language. Poems, prayers, rhymes and songs invite children to line up time and time again, re-entering the language slide. Stutterings, stammerings, slips-of-the-tongue, pauses and mispronunciations are a running and readying, and letting go, a transition from speech's grip to give. Individually and collectively children gradually refine their aural tuning, exercise their auditory imagination. Changing the image from one poem to another, recitations and rhymes and lists and litanies and chants are aural and verbal versions of those:

> ... anglings, aimings, feints
> and squints ...
> all those
> Hunkerings, tensings, pressures of the thumb [tongue]
> Test-outs and pullbacks and re-envisagings ...[4]

All these micro-processes take a poem or a prayer from being an effort to recite that requires concentration to a sheer verbal slide along its verses or lines, an 'at-homeness', a capacity to balance oneself as one negotiates language's slipperiness. It aids the development of an aural sensitivity to discern something of what Heaney means when he speaks of 'the breath of life in the body of sound' and 'the contour of meaning within the pattern of rhythm'.[5] Because it involves its participants *playfully*, this process allows them to embrace – at least now and again – a 'farewell to surefootedness' that plods the solid ground. Such a faring-well is the gift of an imaginative ear that trusts the 'grip' and 'give' of language. The sponsoring of trust in language's intimacy with experience is primary for an education that would encourage us 'a pitch beyond our usual hold upon ourselves'. It is vital for a teaching and learning that from time to time ventures beyond the methodological shallows.

The following teacher's poem is a manifestation of her effort, as teacher, to develop that trust herself. It is a trust that can only come from the ongoing experience of, not so much trying to write 'Poetry' with a capital 'P', as from trying to find an image that can say something as fresh as possible about language. For the teacher, this experience is not to be measured primarily by the success or failure of the poem as poetry. Rather it is about the learning that effort affords and the degree to which it develops the writer's/teacher's capacity to trust in language to surface an image or metaphor adequate to the situation. Only if the teacher genuinely trusts in language can she sponsor her pupils in doing likewise:

Lycro Language
Lycro language
stretches to fit
precisely what

a body needs
to say.
No sagging
of the bottom
line, no bagging
at the knees,
no droopy jowled
vowels,
tongue-in-cheek,
no fear
of falling apart
at the seams.
Velcro-language
fastens meaning in place
temporarily
– as long as needs be.
Then snitch asunder
what words joined together;
for better
or for worse
or for whatever ...[6]

This is not a great poem, but trust is not trust if success is guaranteed. And anyone who has ever tried to 'slide' knows that to fall is part of the experience. In education as in working with poetry and its writing process, failure is resource for learning. But for the teacher to engage with poetry and its writing process is in an educational sense to dig deeper than success and failure. It is to take the risk and give herself over

> ... to the movement of language in which she can never quite steady herself, when the game, as it were, takes over and she is 'suddenly the catcher of a ball'[7]

or the miss-er of the ball, or the slider or faller on a slide, or the skipper or tripper in a rope and so on. It is to attune one's sensitivities to the flirtations of language's seductive invitation into its creative process (remembering that seduction often goes hand in hand with coming-a-cropper.) Even though wary, it is nevertheless to risk the ice 'like a bottle' rather than cling constantly to the surefooted grip of educational grass verges.

Sound-sensing
The following poem, 'Technic-ly Speaking', offers a different example of the sound–sensory qualities of technical–mechanical language as opposed to the more synthetic nature of 'Lycro Language'. The poem was the result of one pupil's fondness for playing with *Lego-Technic*, motivated by a rummage through one of his favorite books – the Argos catalogue. Taking all the technical, mechanical *sounding* words he could find he 'engineered' the following poem.

> **Technic-ly Speaking**
> Answering machine
> Opened the door
> C.D. said 'Hi Fi!'
> Fax relaxed with some micro-chips
> So Micro waved 'bye-bye'.
> She decided to go for a Walkman
> Although she didn't N-intend to
> Then she FAST-Tracked back
> For a Mega Drive
> Around to the Kar-y-out
> O.K. then?
> (Mark, 5th class/P.6)

In the robotic composure, metallic colouring and electronic voice-activation of this poem, one can sense the concentration of a poetry mechanic with bits of words and phrases and machine-parts scattered around his workbench. Technically speaking it is poetry and legitimate enterprise for its author. It is reminiscent of Miroslav Holub who said:

> I like writing for people untouched by poetry; for instance for those who do not even know that it should be at all for them. I would like them to read poems as naturally as they read the papers, or go to a football game.[8]

Children give themselves to the movement of language with the kind of unselfconsciousness Holub is speaking about, a movement whose rhythms and noises are not just of the present, but of the past; not just individual but collective. However, within education there is a risk that, because the visual tends to predominate, the aural may be 'seen' as less important. But the story of poets (whether Greek or Celtic), as has been pointed out, is a story of those who were often, in reality, blind so that they might by 'the antennae of speech see further'.[9] Indeed, this is the story behind Grace's poem:

Poem Switch
I grope for a poem switch
In my head
But it's all dark in there
I can't find the light
To write.
(Grace, 6th class)

It is the story of candles only brought in in order to provide the light by which to 'write down' what the ear of the bardic student had been 'hearing and listening to and fermenting' in the dark. It is the story of images such as the appearance of Fergus, made accessible and memorable by being projected through sound patterns in poetry, rather than through light. It was just such a process that made manifest the Celtic image of education recounted earlier. Oscillation between the voice of Muirgen and the mythical ear of Fergus and vice versa hints at a wavelength on which the unique physical voice of the present may tune in to the broadcasts of the tradition out of which it has arisen, the tradition that is its sponsor. In this respect Robin Flower's notion (sponsored by the invention of telegraphy) that '... those vibrations which are our voices, once surrendered to the air, never come to rest but wander about forever in the ether as potentialities of sound', is an enchanting one. It offers the image of tradition as a sound-potent ether, the kind of thing Ulysses' ear tuned into while his body was tied to the ship's mast, the kind of sound Plato's ear picked up too I suspect, and which might have carried him away had he not trained his eye in a different direction to counteract its power. Taken together with Ted Hughes' conviction that, 'In many people the audial memory is much stronger than the visual. It is wide open to any distinct pattern of sounds. It likes such patterns, and has an extraordinary ability to hang on to them, whether we want to or not'[10] what is being described is the process of the ear attuning itself. A third and critical element that comes into play in this process is darkness. It is in darkness, I believe, that the voice of the present and the ear of tradition attune themselves because it is darkness itself that focuses, sharpens the listening process. Darkness is critical to an educational process that would attune the ear. Education today must – at least some of the time – switch off the light.

Reciting and Performing
The saying or recitation of poetry is an actualisation of these sound-images, which offers an important opportunity for

teacher and pupil to explore the sound sense of poetry, mediating between ear and voice, testing every syllable in, to borrow Hughes' phrase, 'the echo-chamber of the body'. It is a process in which recitation and performance and prayer can generate the possibility of listening in to the collective voice of tradition as well as to the unique voice patterns of particular poets and pray-ers – including the teacher and children themselves. The teacher who understands the value of performing poetry recognises that the essence of real 'elocution' is 'the power or art of appropriate and effective expression' (OED), an art that has nothing to do with imitating upper class or newsreader accents. The opportunity to perform – particularly a poem that is deemed, in the words of Bullock, 'numinous' – is a learning encounter for the child because 'utterance itself imposes a certain minimum form'; indeed the same belief opens the Book of Genesis. Brendan Kennelly's 'Poem from a Three Year Old'[11] makes difficult reading for a primary school child but its dramatic presentation or performance brings to life the three-year-old the poet had in his head when he wrote it. (Kennelly himself remarks of this poem: '… some of my more perceptive critics said they were glad to see I had at last publicly acknowledged my intellectual age!')[12] Children exploring the poem may not fully appreciate, as an adult might, the significance of the questions:

> The dirt you sweep, what happens that,
> What happens all the dirt you sweep
> From flowers and people, what happens all the dirt?
> Is all the dirt what's left of flowers and people …[13]

But children *already know* the child asking the question. They know the constant questioning and search for understanding that the poem embodies, they know its essence. Cyril Cusack puts it thus:

> Let it be said that identification with the poet is the
> most desirable condition for the rendering of true
> poetry, allowing no intrusion of theatricality or
> pretence or even a priority of technical excellence.[14]

And, in this case, to identify with the poet is to identify with
the three-year-old in his imagination. To engage in this kind
of performance of poetry is to 'grope' or feel the body of the
poem, as one might if one were blind. It is to sense through
hearing and speaking the individuality of the poet's voice,
'dramatising' Solzhenitzyn's bugging device. It reveals a
body made of words, sounds, pauses, whispers, inflections,
gestures, pace. It is a process by which the body of language
in the poem is inserted back into the matrix of the
performer's body and in doing so more consciously
savoured in the totality of its sounds, rhythms, meanings
and mysteries. These in return are embodied in a 'knowing-
the-poem-by-heart' in a way similar to that in which
children know their friends and family and may, through the
recitation of prayer, come closer to knowing their God. But
this is not a knowing that children will necessarily be able to
articulate in a formal 'explanation' of what they say, be it
poem or prayer. While it is recognised that children love to
perform spontaneously, the teacher should guard against
cutting the child adrift at the top of the classroom to 'say a
poem for us' without first equipping her with some practice
and resources out of which to build a performance. The
performance of a poem individually or in a group is a
process to be negotiated between the text and the
speaker(s), to be worked through and only eventually
arrived at. The process of arriving, all the while being
thoroughly enjoyed.

Recitation has much in common with elocution and
performance but it is also significantly different. The
difference arises out of its historical and cultural

background in Irish society as well as its etymological links with the music of 'recital'. The OED defines 'recitation' as 'A musical declamation, intermediate between singing and ordinary speech …' and the verb 'to recite' as 'To repeat or utter aloud (something previously heard or learned by heart), to repeat to an audience from memory'. This narrative mediation from memory between ordinary speech and song is exemplified in the ballad form, an especially intrinsic part of the literary tradition of these islands. It resides within the tradition of bards, folksingers, balladeers, sheet sellers, fleadh ceoil and so on. Its mediatory role is particularly useful in exploring poetry because it provides a bridge for the story between prose and free verse; a bridge for the voice between spoken and sung, between oral and written; and in the past has provided a sociological bridge between those whose tradition has been oral, non-literate, working class and those of a literate upper class. John Montague has said of Irish 'versification':

> These anonymous songs are the true achievement of Anglo-Irish poetry in the nineteenth century … 'When the Irish language was fading … the Irish street ballad in English was the half-way house between the Irish culture and the new English way'. Their influence on our two greatest modern writers, Yeats and Joyce, show that they can be a taproot for the most gifted.[15]

In this way recitation complements performance by putting the child in touch with the dynamics of oral tradition that issue in sound and its structures in the 'ether-eal' of the collective past. It also embeds the ear with sounds, cadences and rhythms. Although it must be acknowledged of course that not all material for recitation must be drawn from the past just as not all material for performance will be contemporary. Performing and reciting are acts of 'pure vocal duration', exercising the muscles of the voice, the ear and the memory as they vibrate off one another. Children – especially in a group – delight in a poem's saying as a celebration of the achievement of breathing and blowing a two-dimensional formula on a page into a three-dimensional, quivering, meaningful bubble-of-breath, reminiscent again of the act of creation in the Book of Genesis. As part of bringing a particular poem to life, the process of reading and re-reading is also a process of what was once called 'saying it into yourself', a process through which one becomes receptive to language. The Kingman Report highlights the importance of this process:

> Such a reception of language allows the individual greater possibilities of production of language.[16]

This is not just true of the English curriculum however; it is also true of the religion curriculum. The purpose of stories, conversations, poems, prayers, all the language elements of a religion programme is, I believe, less about teaching a moral, or making a point, or arriving at a conclusion or claiming a belief than it is about immersing the child deeper and deeper into language. It is about allowing her greater and deeper possibilities in relation to expressing experience, experience that at its deepest may be religious. Religious education's primary concern must be to nourish receptivity to language and religious language which will allow greater possibilities for production of *fresh* religious language. It also, needless to say, applies to the teacher and her own reading and writing. The following is an example of how the teacher as learner-writer can build her own bridges, for herself and her classes, between past and present, but also between curriculum content as something that is to be found outside oneself and one's class, and that which is available within oneself. This poem was written as a gesture towards the tradition of November as the month of 'All Souls' in an effort to say something small but significant to young children about death and dying. If, as Hughes suggested, poetry tries to get at 'the crowiness of the crow', the essence of this poem lies in the 'storyness of the story'. It also verifies the above statement of the Kingman Report because it became stuck at a critical stage in its writing, and might lie unfinished, even today were it not for a borrowed rhyme from Heaney's translation of the Russian poet Jan Kochanowski's 'Lament 8', specifically – 'The void that fills my house is so intense/Now that my girl is gone. It baffles sense'.[17] It is based on a version of a story in the saint-lore of *Beasts and Saints* by Helen Wadell.[18]

Columba and the Sean-Chapall Bán

Most stories begin with beginnings,
    This story begins with the end
Of an old man's life on an island
    And a horse's 'Goodbye' to his friend.

One Saturday morning Columba
    Woke up in bed and just knew
That this, the last day of the week,
    Was going to be his last day too.

He jumped out of bed, determined,
    It being the day that was in it,
To continue his life, as he had always done,
    Living – to the very last minute.

Resting his head in his hands he prayed,
    'Buíochas le Dia go deo!
Molaimid thú, Móraimid thú
    Thall 's abhus 's anseo'.

Patting the pillow, 'Goodbye Bed', he said,
   'In you I have known "rest-in-peace",
No matter how dark or dreary the night
   You cradled me, 'rís 's arís'.

'Goodbye Window,' he said, opening it wide,
'You brought fresh air and light to my life.
You helped me breathe. You helped me see
   Through trouble and struggle and strife.'

'Goodbye Room,' he said, closing the door,
'You gave me space just to be
On my own, or with you when I needed
   Just the two of us, you room, and me.'

Neither Bed, Window, nor Room
   Moved nor uttered a word,
But the old saint knew (as old saints do)
   That each one had listened and heard.

It was May, the first month of summer,
   Columba's last of the year,
His friends were at work in the Western fields,
   They stopped as the old man drew near.

'I have this notion,' Columba said,
   'Don't ask me how, what, or why –
But I know in my heart; I feel in my bones,
It's time; time for goodbye.'

'Where are you going?' they asked in alarm.
   'I'm going away', he replied.
'I won't be back – but I'll see you around,
   If you know what I mean', he smiled.

That said, he opened the doors of the barn
    And blessed its stores of grain,
'Tá Dia maith! You'll not want for food
    When I'm gone', he repeated again.

Tired, though not yet quite finished
    Columba sat down for a rest
On an old mill-stone by the side of the road.
    'Brother Diarmuid,' he said, 'Have you guessed?'

'Guessed what Brother?' Diarmuid his friend asked.
    'I feel cross; yet I'm sad deep inside.
You talk of goodbye, of going away,
    What is it you're trying to hide?'

Just at that moment, his Sean-Chapall Bán
    With head drooping low in dismay,
Plodded along to Columba and stood
    Bereft, of whinny or neigh.

Silent she stood there, her wise old eyes
    Filled with sorrow intense.
She knew her old friend was going to die
    Though *how* she knew – that baffles sense!

In silence the saint stroked her forehead,
    Her eyes filled with tears to the brim,
They spilled over, rolled down her cheeks
    And dropped from her quivering chin.

'Your tears are upsetting my brother,
    Imigh leat!' Diarmuid protested.
'Let her be,' sighed Columba, 'this dumb creature knew
    Though you had not even guessed it.

She senses that I am dying.
   I *told* you – else you wouldn't know.
This creature's natural horse-sense
   Is a wonder, God has bestowed.'

A last look to Ireland, then back to Iona
   Where he had come to reside,
As the Sean-Chapall turned and ambled away
   Columba lay down, and just died.

Yes, Columba just lay down and died
   At rest, in peace, Amen.
Now this story reaches its beginning
   Because death is never the end.[19]

To recite poems such as these particularly when the verses are shared out among a class and the whole poem is 'put back together again' by the coming together of the individuals a class or group recitation, is to 'evoke', rather than 'teach', the noises, rhythms and rhymes of the ballad form, such as Yeats's 'The Ballad of Father Gilligan', or William Allingham's 'Up The Airy Mountain', uniting the say-er and the said in much the same unity as the dancer and the dance. The memorising that happens through recitation of bits of ballads such as 'The Old Woman of the Roads' or 'Pangur Bán' leads children not just into knowing the words of the poem, but into the collective memory of the tradition, in this instance the literary folk tradition, the 'home-made' poems of their people. It is a past which for children begins with that which is just over their shoulder, with parents and grandparents. Children discover to their delight that their 'people' know and can recite these same ballads. These poems

> ... g[i]ve verse, however humble, a place in the life of the home, ma[k]e it one of the ordinary rituals of life[20]

like the place recitation of the rosary used to have. They bring it within Bullock's current of normal life, give parents and children experience of a mutually affirming bond and identity an increasingly rare phenomenon in today's curriculum. Recitation and the ballad form (and previously prayer) fall within 'the hearth culture'.[21] For the teacher/ learner/writer to be a member of 'the hearth culture' is to be one of those who tend the fire, who are vigilant and skilled in the 'art' of lighting, keeping, fuelling or rekindling a fire, a dying art. To foster the poetic hearth culture is to be vigilant with regard to poetry's fire, and for the teacher–writer its fire within education and religious education.

The ballad form can do much to kindle poetry within the life of the school. Its sturdy rhythms, formal patterns, 'chunky' verses and strong rhymes are hefty blocks – a kind of poetic 'Lego' – for working with. Children compose, as Ezra Pound might have redefined it in another instance, more so 'in sequence of a metronome' than a musical phrase. In its distance from the rhythms of everyday speech, it often reflects more of a cartoon-type reality than complex human reality. It is a kind of poetic puppetry, a form entirely appropriate to a poem celebrating the visit of the School Clown, an event in the real life of the school that, attuned by the ear and the voice, gave a live connection into the ballad tradition and became:

The Puppet Man
The puppet man with his puppet clan
Came to our school today.
He said, 'Well hello! Will you come see my show?'
We said 'Ready! Steady! Let's go!'

A wig and a hat, a joke and a chat,
A song and a clap and a bow;

There was laughter and after the water got squirted
We giggled and sniggled, 'What now?'

Said Mark, 'What the heck 'bout a sword through the
neck,
It's only a trick so I'll try it!'
His laugh sounded hollow, he tried not to swallow
Now all of a sudden Mark's quiet!

Behind the striped canvas, the puppets lay handless
Awaiting their turn to impress us,
Which they did more and more and we shouted 'Encore!'
Now he's gone with his puppets God bless us!
(And them too)
(5th/6th class/P.7)

Nor does the ballad form restrict itself to local events but it
can cast its web of sound to catch events on the other side of
the world and bring them 'home', as in:

Living Room
I was watching the telly
And on came the news.
I saw these black children,
No food, no clothes, no shoes.
I thought, 'This is awful
I'll put a stop to that',
I went in the telly
Made a friend
Had a chat.

'Come out here
To my living room with me,
You can share some of my clothes
And I'll give you your tea.

I'm sure my jeans would fit you
And my other runners – size two,
And sausage, beans and chips for tea
Will that be O.K. for you?'

'What's your name?
Where do you live?
Where do you go to school?
Who's your best friend?
When is your birthday?
Would you like to go to the pool?
Do you like Madonna?
Did you see 'Home Alone'?
What age are your brothers and sisters?
Have you not got a bike?
What team do you like?
Isn't it better living here?
Sure stay ... go on ... '
But she only said
in a whispery voice

'I want
to go home'.
(3rd/4th class/P.5/6)

Attuning the ear of a child has significant complexities, hinted at by George Steiner who notes that:

> In most societies and throughout history the status of women has been akin to that of children. Both groups are maintained in a condition of privileged inferiority. Both suffer obvious modes of exploitation – sexual, legal, economic – while benefiting from a mythology of special regard. Under sociological and psychological pressure, both minorities have developed internal

codes of communication and defense. There is a language world of women as there is of children.[22]

Consequently, since the thrust of the language of sub-cultures such as childhood may often be geared more towards concealment than revelation, attuning the ear of the child requires a sensitivity built on respect for and interest in the learner's language; it requires that the teacher

> take the trouble to hear the actual language of the child, to receive and interpret its signals without distorting them.[23]

As an example, the rhyme in the first verse of 'The Puppet Man' overshoots its runway a little in the first verse. When I read that first verse now I remember the curriculum's caution about the use of rhyme in composition and I wonder why I did not work with the class to correct the rhyme structure to make it fit properly. But something, perhaps ignorance, or lack of poetic competence, or perhaps intuition, stopped me. Most poems are written by adults for children rather than *by* children *for* children and in the sub-cultural world that is childhood, rhyme and structure may not be what it is in the adult world. When I read that poem now, I wonder if overshooting the runway is due to an excited revving of rhyme and rhythm's engines in the words 'man' and 'clan'. These are held in a steady thrum by the heavy meter, like a diesel engine ticking noisily over, running on the spot as it were. But they begin to gather impetus in 'hello', 'show' and after 'Ready', and 'Steady', 'Go' is the only possibility; it is the expression of the poem's lift off! It is this excitement that carries the taxiing poem, tilting it towards poetic form, giving it lift off in the first place. Overshooting the runway is therefore entirely appropriate for this poem. After all, the sounds made by any child who plays with a plane or car or train show that they know the difference between the sound their engines make as they are getting going is utterly different to those that they make when they are well underway. It would have been wrong of me to try to 'fix' this poem's first verse, but only my ear could tell me so. Similarly, the disintegration of the rhyme structure at the end of 'Living Room' described a kind of running out of steam or a landing rhyme short of the runway as it appropriate for the 'dunt' received by the child wanting to go home despite the luxuries available.

Ted Hughes offers sound advice for teachers with regard to their role in the attuning process, and in developing what this thesis has called aural intelligence and imagination. He points out that:

> What is essential, then ... is to keep the audial faculty wide open, and not so much look at the words as listen for them – listening as widely, deeply and keenly as possible, testing every whisper on the air in the echo-chamber of your whole body.[24]

The audial faculty, which is only partly a conscious faculty and partly a 'hidden sense', a 'deep pocket', a religious faculty, is kept open in a particular way through the intermingling of the playfulness of children and the playfulness of language.

> We learn the language in the first place by being irresistibly drawn into it as into a game (in Merleau–Ponty's words, 'the whole of the spoken language surrounding the child snaps him up like a whirlwind, tempts him by its internal articulations'), and it is as an extension of this game that the language itself develops ... the life of language consists in the constant playing further of the game that we began when we first learned to speak.[25]

This understanding of the play-full relationship between language and learning and life are crucial to primary education. It suggests to me that primarily education is about drawing children further and further into the language game. Plato, as has already been pointed out, was suspicious of play, concluding from his observations of the way in which children could be slaves one minute and freemen the next, that it risked preparing children to be subversive of the social order. In more recent times, play has been seen as efficacious, as preparation for adult role-taking, or, in more specific contexts, as directly educational in promoting the development of mathematical, social and scientific concepts. Although they might appear in opposition, both these views of play share a common assumption i.e. that play is a *means*, a means to achieve, or subvert the achievement, of particular ends. In this way play is being understood as rationally employed strategy. However play that is genuine 'holds the player in its spell, draws him into play and keeps him there'.[26] The poetic process of attuning the ear through play is subversive of the scientific–rational order of much of education's aims and methodologies whether that be in general or in religious education. Any teacher who has observed children at play recognises when the child is taken up and transformed and becomes happily subordinate to the game or the 'play' itself. When this happens it is the kind of play referred to in Heaney's already quoted 'Markings', 'effort in another [educational] world'. It is this kind of playful effort in this other-than-scientifically-rational world that produces 'Trying It On' as Grace (2nd class) did:

Trying It On
One day I made myself a poem.
I tried it on.
I looked in the mirra.

The buttons were done up
Wrong.

Or learning to cycle as David (5th class) did:

Trying To Cycle A Bike
I pedal an idea
Round and round
In my head.

I try to steer it
Along.

Words
Spokes
Pencils
Verses
Spinning, spinning, spinning.
Round and round
On my page
My poem
Getting nowhere fast.[27]

or going swimming as Catriona (5th class) did:

Swimming In Poetry
Can you jump into a poem
Like you jump into a pool
Or do you sit on the edge
And dabble your words
A toe or two at a time?

or toying with a loose tooth as Tara (4th class) did:

Shaky Tooth
A shaky tooth
And a pushy tongue

Just cannot leave
Each other alone.
It's coming ... coming
Coming ... OUT!
It's all red.
I thought it was all white.[28]

These poems recollect experiences stored in and through play, harvesting them by ear through poetry.

So far this section has concentrated on fostering an aural intelligence, nourishing what Cox meant when he spoke of children's instinctive pleasure in rhythm, pattern and rhyme. But the experienced teacher–writer must also be alert to anything in a child's writing that she recognises instinctively as true sounding aspects of an already existing aural sensitivity in a pupil. For example, Dónal's poem was one which the teacher happened to come across in his copy. It had, apparently, been written in response to a story about a dragon in his reading book.

What is interesting about it is the child's deft handling of rhythm, pattern and rhyme, a handling that reveals an *a priori* sensitivity or intelligence with regard to these matters. Most striking is the poem's form – the fact that it begins and ends with the same two lines. This dragon has certain form. In his head and in his tail, he knows who he is and where he comes from. The powerful body of sound, in rhyme and rhythm and repetition of 'I' suggests that this dragon's remarkable sense of identity may well reflect its writer's sense of self. It is a poem that reveals something of this seven-year-old's ear for sound, rhythms and patterns of language and the capacity to craft these into poetic form reminiscent of Edward Lear's work. Of course as teacher, one would echo the Primary Curriculum view concerning 'an over-preoccupation with rhyme leading to mere doggerel at the expense of any real self-expression', but a poem such

as the one in question is not so much about 'self-expression' as setting the 'self' echoing, to paraphrase Heaney. It is a poem which is all about giving language 'a good rattle', literally shaking the living rhythms and rhymes out of it! It strikes out unselfconsciously like the fist of the infant striking by accident the string of beads and baubles stretched across the pram. Or, to change the image, rhythms and rhymes are the 'big noises' of children's poetry; they are the clump–clop of little feet enjoying big shoes; they are the means whereby the young child tries poetry on. Accidentally too (it is unlikely to have been intentional on the part of the child) the rhyming of dragon and Lagan surfaced in the teacher/reader an image of Twelfth of July parades and marches as the annual appearance of a dragon which is to some a carnival creature, and to others a mythical monstrosity. What was of greater concern to the teacher however was how she might nourish the already existing craft and gift in this young poet. Given that, sound-wise, there was no more to be done to, or for, the poem, she decided, following Bullock's advice to have this child's work 'emerge from the covers of the exercise book',[29] to have it illustrated so that it might grow in status in the experience of its creator from something 'stuck in his copy' to something he might hang on his bedroom wall. There is of course another side to this coin because to have the poem illustrated is to superimpose form on the image in the poet's and the reader's own imagination from the adult outside. On the one hand this is undoubtedly adult interference and is questionable; on the other hand, the young teacher's own need for confirmation may be at work here too. Given the potentially subversive nature of poetry and its writing process within education, she may have needed the consolation/confirmation of the pretty picture more than the child. But who's who and what's what are, like teaching and learning, fluid and flow in and out of each other and nowhere more so than in the infant classroom. Confirmation may have been needed somewhat.

In the end, attuning the ear is a process critical to language as sound rather than as visual written word, and poetry is its finest embodiment. For religious educators, an attuned ear and an auditory imagination is vital if one is to hear the voice of that God of the Old Testament who was constantly talking to people, or to heed the urgent injunction of the parabler to 'listen then if you have ears'. The process of attuning the ear and the voice are educationally and religiously therefore not only about the written and read, but challenge the dominance in our modern scientific and technological world of the written word over the spoken which 'is a further stage in the process whereby speech itself is abstracted from its matrix in the whole body';[30] in other words, a situation in which word is made less flesh. Counterpointing the Greek image of education as one in which light, the visual and the eye are paramount, the process of attuning the ear is one that, like fermentation, is carried out in the dark and is integral to a Celtic-poetic notion of education.

> In ... language verbal sounds are organically linked to the vast system of root meanings and related associations, deep in the subsoil of psychological life, beyond our immediate awareness or conscious manipulation. It is the distinction of poetry to create strong patterns in these hidden meanings as well as the clearly audible sounds. The hidden patterns are, if anything, much the stronger. The audial memory picks up those patterns in the depths from what it hears at the surface.[31]

Preparation for this level of aural imagination, or intelligence, or sensitivity, is rehearsed through activities such as the repetition of prayers, mantras, chants and so on as well as by the performance and recitation of poetry, whose importance is underlined by Cox: 'Children ... should experience and take part in the performance of poetry',[32] but is endorsed more fully by the religious education curriculum:

> In the saying of poems and prayers the child is holding a kind of aural mirror up to her or his ear ... [thereby hearing] his or herself reflected in sound, cadence, and rhythm ... of the language of the present day community and the communities that preceded it. The child may [then] begin to develop an aural dimension to her or his aural imagination ... These are the opportunities that it is the duty of any religion programme aimed at enhancing fullness of life to offer.[33]

Attuning the ear is just one of the micro-processes of poetry's writing process. And while it has been focused on in this chapter, the extent to which it can or should be isolated from other micro parts is limited since there is constant inter-play between all the parts or dynamics. Language is a messy, fluid business but this is as it should be since play and messiness are at the heart of childhood and of the primary school classroom. Learning is an ongoing inter-play of the child's development of language and language's development of the child. The playfulness of language and play in the life of the child are not two discrete activities but one continuous movement like the ocean's motion, a motion in which experience plays through language and language plays through experience. It is a continuous sing-song.

Notes

1. *The Cox Report*, p. 150.
2. *Cox on Cox*, p. 80.
3. *Seeing Things*, p. 86.
4. Ibid.
5. In 'Learning From Eliot', *Seamus Heaney Fiftieth Birthday Issue*, Agenda Publications, 1989.
6. In Patterson, G., *Things Made and Things Said*, Belfast, The Stranmillis Press, 1999, p. 107.
7. *Back to the Rough Ground*, p. 152.
8. Heaney, *The Government of the Tongue*, London, Faber, 1988, p. 47.
9. *After Babel*, p. 24.
10. *The School Bag*, p. 567.
11. In *Irish Poems For Young People*, Quinn, B., Cashman, S. (eds), Dublin, Wolfhound Press, 1982, p. 84.
12. Kennelly, B., 'The Roaring Storm Of Your Words' in Richard Pine (ed.), *Dark Fathers Into Light*, Northumberland, Bloodaxe Books, 1994, p. 181.
13. 'Poem from a Three Year Old' from *A Time for Voices: Selected Poems 1960-1990*, Bloodaxe Books, 1990.
14. In *Lifelines: Letters from famous people about their favourite Poem*, Dublin, Town House and Country House, 1992, p. 56.
15. Montague, J., in the introduction to *The Faber Book of Irish Verse*, London, Faber, 1974, pp. 33–4.
16. *Report of the Committee of Enquiry into the Teaching of English Language*, Department Of Education and Science, London, H.M.S.O., Chapter 2:21.
17. From *Laments,* translated by Seamus Heaney and Stanislaw Baranczak, London, Faber, 1995, p. 17.
18. London, Constable and Company, 1934, pp. 46–9.
19. Published in *Alive-O 3*, Dublin: Veritas, 1998.
20. *Preoccupations,* p. 27.
21. From an interview with Fintan O'Toole in *The Irish Times*, Saturday, 10 October 1999.
22. *After Babel*, p. 38.
23. Ibid.
24. Hughes and Heaney, *The School Bag*, London, Faber, 1997, p. 568.
25. *Back to the Rough Ground*, p. 150.

26. Ibid., p. 136.
27. Published in *The Top Dog*, Dublin, O'Brien Press, 1997.
28. Ibid.
29. *A Language for Life*, Chap. 11.15, p. 164.
30. Dunne also notes that … 'even though silent reading is now the stock response to writing, the written word is dead unless the reader can convert it into (at least virtual) speech – a speech, moreover, which is itself dead unless it carries a whole range of emphasis and inflection which is not registered on the page. As Collingwood says of words on the page (and this includes technical terms which are indeed purged of emotional expressiveness precisely as part of their becoming technical, but which acquire expressiveness the moment they are taken into use): "If you don't know what tone to say them in, you can't say them at all: they are not words" … expressiveness is an ineliminable feature of all language. (An attempt to eliminate it is, indeed part of the process whereby language becomes intellectualised – i.e. modified to serve the purposes of thinking – but while language can allow this attempt to introduce a not altogether disruptive tension into itself, it cannot allow it to succeed fully: it retains its function as language only insofar as the intellectualisation is incomplete.)' *Back to the Rough Ground*, p. 66.
31. *The School Bag*, p. 568.
32. *The Cox Report*, p. 80.
33. *Alive-O 6*, Introduction, Veritas, 2002, p. 36.

6 The Writing Teacher

Having made her own way into poetry, the teacher must begin to work with the clues that the experience has given her as to how to nurture the poetic in the young child. By giving shape in her own writing to her own experience, the teacher can develop herself as writer and takes up that role assigned to her by the Cox Report of actively modeling the success the student strives for. To illustrate this point, the two poems that follow were written by the teacher about small everyday happenings in the life of her Junior/Senior Infant or P.1/P.2 classes. They are an attempt to present an image of poetry and the process of poem-making based on the teacher's observation of pupils' own experience of 'creation'.

All Foll Down

Can this be called a poem? It hardly seems like the sort of thing one would find in a children's anthology – *The Oxford First Poetry Book* series, for example – or even in the 'whackier' works of writers such as Colin McNaughton or Michael Rosen or Roger McGough. When can one call a piece of writing a poem and when not? This is a key worry for the uncertain teacher/writer/learner and is the twin of another question the teacher will ask herself: 'Is this learning?', especially in relation to the deeper dimensions of education which resist the usual assessment measures. Such questions will become the focus of much of her attention. This learning is already intimately linked with language, and insofar as the teacher (or pupil) would 'learn' when something can or cannot be called a poem she must challenge those assessment methods modeled on scientific or instrumental reasoning. Such methods cannot offer comfort to the teacher in her uncertainty and insecurity in relation to what is or isn't poetry. But uncertainty is a condition of human existence that teaching as an activity involving human relations cannot take flight from. Nor is poetry itself immune from anxiety – even Heaney acknowledges that in the case of one of his first attempts at a poem as he says:

> I hadn't even the guts to put my name to it. I called myself *Incertus*, uncertain, a shy soul fretting and all that.[1]

The question of when a piece is or isn't a poem is also a question of how poetry is made, a question that is central to this book. This poem is built; it is built out of the idea of 'poetry as child's play' or, perhaps more accurately, building on the idea of the raw, crude material in the child's play as potential poetry, this poem plays on the fairly common image, represented pictorially and literally, of words as building blocks. It crudely constructs them into an appropriately 'wobbly' poem. The wobbly nature of the poem arises as much from the writer's uneasiness in playing with words and toying with poetry in this seemingly childishly poetic way as from the actual children's building of the blocks themselves. But play is the legitimate business of the infant's classroom and indeed of all primary school classrooms and because it is so these are the classrooms that represent postmodern educational process at its healthiest. That children should play is less contentious however than that teachers should play around with the teaching–learning process. Without an – albeit nervous – willingness on the part of the teacher to 'play around', this poem would not have been written/drawn/built; in short, 'expressed'. Pupils whose teacher is not prepared to play with language, words and images are at a serious disadvantage in terms of their linguistic, social, religious development – in short their

human development, not to mention the development of the teacher and *her* capacity to be 'both the door and what comes through it'. Words and images are the literal building blocks of this poem; play is the process by which it was made. The poem represents the young child's experience of *literally* playing with language, playing with words, playing with images. It also represents the experience of playing in the game that is language itself. The playing of that language-experience game is crucial to primary education whether religious or general because in essence, when one truly plays, one freely places oneself in a situation in which I as player do not have control but am caught up or give myself up to something bigger than myself, bigger than all those playing, that is, the game itself. What is crucial in relation to play (and in relation to language-play) is 'the primacy of the play over the consciousness of the player'.[2]

It is exactly this primacy that establishes itself when a teacher and her class play with words in poetry and its writing process. Nor, it seems to me, is this 'primacy of play over the consciousness of the player/s' all that different from the state of relations that exists between the biblical notion of kingdom and the experience of situations in which it 'comes' – given its similarity to the dynamics of play it is hardly surprising that children exemplify belonging-in-it. Kingdom is the presence of a playful God. The primacy of the play-process in poetry is that it opens a space within education where both the student and teacher may enter:

> But when one *has* entered, then 'all playing is a being played ... The real subject of the game ... is not the player [writer] but instead the game [writing] itself. The game is what holds the player in its spell, draws him into play and keeps him there.[3]

Classrooms in which poetry is played with are at risk of being deeply subversive of the instrumentalist bias of modern thought whether that thought is applied to religious education or education generally. But their subversion is positive, not negative because 'art is shown to be best understood as a "transformation" of play and play is claimed to reach its highest perfection in art'.[4] This statement is at the heart of what I believe Picasso meant. When he said that 'every child is an artist', I believe it is true because every child is a player.

In the teacher's handling of this poem's presiding image there is a definite 'wobbling', reflecting the children's handling of the building blocks. In the teacher's nervous handling of the poetry-building process she also reflects the nervous excitement of her young pupils as they build their tower. And at another level this poem's nervous wobble is a literal representation of the tension between art and the reality it inhabits, in this case the professional reality of the teacher and the playful reality of the children, 'indeed tension seems to be necessarily part and parcel of the best creative efforts'.[5] And yet another dimension to the tension in this poem comes from the state of the 'power-relations' in primary education, i.e. teachers and pupils (most likely, women and children) giving themselves to the movement of language and poetry-writing's potential subversion of education's technically-speaking surefooted order. What constitutes this poem's wobble and its writer/teacher's mental 'stumbling block' is this exact tension; but it is in holding this tension that the poem *succeeds as a poem*. Its presiding image – the building of construction blocks – functions as an effective image holding three different events in playful tension. It overlays the child's unsteady hand playing with building bricks with the teacher's unsteady 'hand-ling' of poetry writing, while at the same time under-laying both of these with the image of words as building blocks and the whole process and structure of the poem as a play on building itself. Its authenticity as a poem lies in the playful hands involved in the process of building their blocks so tall and so precariously that they *tease* Structure and Form, tease the Spirit of Creation, enticing it to become involved. The first sign of a wobble is the moment in which that spirit can no longer resist the temptation. The building or game has taken on a life of its own. All those involved – the spirit of the game and the children – anticipate that final delightful collapse and new beginning; the essential head-over-heels involvement of order and chaos in life, order and chaos in learning.

> **painting**
> paintbrush tickles page
> until hole giggles
> its way through
> painting wetting itself
> with the laughing

This second poem is the result of the teacher's observation of her Junior Infant class's first painting session of the year. The merging of product and process – the actual painting and the act of painting – is reflected in the poem's gramatically blurred, unpunctuated form. These blurred edges hint at the fusion of the painter and the painting. At no stage is a definite product, a picture, mentioned; the word 'painting' functions as both verb and noun. It fuses 'doing-the-naming' and 'naming-the-doing'. Just as a water-colour blends colours, in this poem the various elements of the experience – the brush, the page, the laughter, the hole – are water-coloured together in a fluid unity. The poem's form appears like the image on a photograph out of its developing solution, like Creation out of a misty Genesis. It expresses the blurring dilation and dilution of a particularly *engaged* knowledge. Engaged knowledge is knowledge that quivers, like the bubble quivers in the breath of the blower, just before it detaches from the wand.

This poem was not planned in advance; like the hole, knowledge and understanding only gradually appeared out of it as it was 'happening'. It was written by the teacher, quickly, as part of that process of focusing and refocusing attention on a blurred impression she had as she observed the pupils that 'something' was happening; she wrote the poem in order to see more clearly what that 'something' might be. If it is true that

> People who don't paint ... like to fancy that everybody ... sees just as much as an artist sees, and that the artist only differs in having the technical accomplishment of painting what he sees. But that is nonsense ... a good painter paints things because until he has painted them he doesn't know what they are like,[6]

then the teacher too may write in order to see, educationally, what is going on. This kind of writing (more so than doing notes) is the kind of writing that is critical for an education that would seek to understand 'what it's at'. The knowledge and understanding that arose through the writing process is relevant to the children for whom the poem was written, offering as it does a way for them to begin to understand their experience of painting. But, it also offers the teacher knowledge and understanding *about the kind of teacher she is*, the way in which she understands education, and painting's and poetry's role within it. It is not that the aim of writing poetry is to make the teacher, in the words of Donald Schon, a 'reflective practitioner', but, because the process of writing engages her linguistically and experientially, this is, in effect, what she *learns* to become. In this way the teacher's learning is intimately bound up with that of her young pupils and with language and the writing process; with revelation not just of the self to the self, but of the teacher to the teacher and the classroom community to the classroom community.

The Cox Report points to the various roles the teacher will take up in fostering children as real writers when it says:

> They [teachers] will be observers, facilitators, modellers, readers and supporters.[7]

Incision
Massive Ferguson
unzips the chest of the hill;
gulls like white corpuscles
spill into the sky.

This poem was written by the teacher in the role of 'modeler' of the success the pupil strives for. It is a poem that presents diverse particulars – ploughing, tractor, hill unzipping, chest, gulls, flight and so on 'in a newly designed arrangement'.[8] Its usefulness as an example of the writing process lies in the example it offers of the making of an image by creating new metaphor. The meaning of 'ploughing' is extended by comparing it to an 'unzipping'; juxtaposing this unzipping with 'the chest of the hill' combines the two into new meaning. By a similar metaphoric process in the last two lines, gulls – a relatively common and concrete 'vehicular image' – are identified with white corpuscles, less well known as an observable part of everyday reality. The poem then goes on to create new meaning by arranging or synthesising the white corpuscles and gulls with 'spill into the sky'. This arrangement is facilitated by the already existing associations of spilling with blood, but immediately dislocates any presuppositions by reversing the direction of that spill – towards the sky rather than towards the earth. Taken together, these two metaphors constitute a single 'oeuvre': the unzipping and the spilling are linked and joined in the poem's presiding image of ploughing. It is a poem in the Imagist tradition, which concerned itself with poetry as accurate description of reality despite the criticisms of Imagists that 'Poem after poem in this sort is full of the simple wonder of a child ... The big-eyed recognition is about as far toward correlation of their material as the Imagists ... ever get'.[9] Despite these adult concerns, the Imagist tradition has much to offer the child and the teacher in terms of the writing process and vice-versa (as indeed the child has much to offer the Imagist tradition). It encourages close observation, focused thinking and careful description. Besides, one wonders whether the poetry in any poem lies more in its complexity than in its simplicity. In the case of the poem in question, its simplicity is of immense value, especially for children who live close to and, in many cases, make their living directly off the land.

The central metaphor of the poem – ploughing – is a routine, common-sense, unemotional operation. Its clinical nature is reflected in the poem's curt-cut title 'Incision', a purposeful and carefully calculated opening-up as opposed to a rough gash. What is being expressed is the nature of this routine 'agri-surgical' operation. The poem simply presents an image and leaves it at that, allowing the reader the freedom to take it or leave it too.

At another level this poem describes a symbolic wound – a common symbol for poetry itself. The wound in this case is not a very deep one, which may suggest that the writer has not yet developed the poetic capacity to dig deep into poetry's underground. Or its shallowness may be in respect of the childhood context in which the poem was written; the turning over of the topsoil may be deep enough for children yet. One senses however that those white corpuscles spilling into the heavens may be the symbolic fruits of 'massive' effort on the part of the writer. Certainly the 'massive' in the opening line is very much out of proportion with the ease of effort in unzipping and spilling. If poetry is 'a revelation of the self to the self', then this poem may reveal to the writer something in herself of the relationship between poetry as 'gift' and poetry as 'hard work' as a kind of 'ploughing along'. However, bear in mind the caution that:

> It is dangerous for the writer to become too self-conscious about his own processes: to name them too definitively may have the effect of confining them to what is named. A poem always has elements of accident about it ... there is always a risk in conducting your own inquest: you might begin to believe the coroner in yourself rather than put your trust in the man in you who is capable of the accident.[10]

The experience of having written this poem quite quickly or having 'dug it up' allows a greater possibility of recognising either the 'gift' or the 'hard work' in pupils' writing. In a religious educational context too, it offers an opportunity to wonder about the extent to which the parables of the poetic-teacher Jesus had elements of 'divine' accident about them. Does the casualness of verbs such as 'sowing'/'scattering', 'finding', hint at a reluctance to be overly self-conscious about his own creative processes, preferring to credit the Creator in himself, and leave the inquest to others? If so, perhaps primary teaching generally can model his approach.

Notes

1. *Preoccupations*, p. 13.
2. *Back to the Rough Ground*, p. 134. Dunne comments further that 'Play ... can most deeply subvert the instrumentalist bias of modern thought, i.e., the tendency to think of unimpeded "subjects" achieving their pre-planned "ends" through the efficacy of methodical "means" which they are able to put at their disposal. And language is the all-encompassing reality which, to the extent that we succeed in reflecting on it, shows more deeply and with more universal import than anything else the limits of instrumentalist or method-based rationality.'
3. Ibid.
4. Ibid.
5. *Things Made and Things Said*, p. 10.
6. *Back to the Rough Ground*, p. 72.
7. *The Cox Report*, Chap. 10.15, p. 147; See also 2.5.
8. Wheelwright, P., *Metaphor and Reality*, Bloomington, Indiana University Press, p. 81.
9. *Poems In the Making*, pp. 33–4.
10. *Preoccupations*, p. 52.

7 Close Reading

The teacher, as also the pupil, as also the poet, live within a community, be it an educational community or a local community, such as is the subject of Bríd's poem:

> Would you live in Stabannon if you had the choice?
> There's the school there's the pub
> There's the church and the youth club
> And then there's Richard
> Stabannon's main man
> Who'll hold his head high
> Just to show that he can.
> Would you live in Stabannon
> If you had the choice?
> (Bríd, 5th class/P.7)

On first reading, Bríd's poem about her locality seems rather slight, a poem that never really got going, a poem that doesn't immediately grab the reader's attention (perhaps because its writing hasn't grabbed the *writer's* attention). This teacher response is interesting in itself and will be the subject of attention later in this section but for now it is enough to follow the advice offered by James Britton:

> ... very close reading of children's writing is essential because that is the best means we have of understanding their writing processes.[1]

Close reading is in itself another micro-part of the process of poetry writing – not just for the teacher as reader of the pupil's material, but also for the pupil as reader of her own (and other's) material. The image of 'very close reading' suggests a movement on the part of the reader from a position that is at a distance or at a remove from the text, to a position much closer in – in fact *into* – it, a movement that again is carried out in language. At the heart of the matter of close-reading of texts – children's or otherwise – lies hermeneutics and the question of 'distance' from a text. In the context of the usual set of power relations within which a teacher reads a pupil's text – an essay, or story, for example – there will often be the assumption of a recognised authoritative vantage point outside or over against the text that the teacher might suppose himself to be in possession of. The teacher, it may be assumed, knows 'how' to read the text, understand it, and from the objective standpoint of some professionally acquired set of literary-critical criteria, make judgements in relation to its quality. But reaching an understanding of a pupil's poem is not something the teacher can 'work out' in this way, i.e. in the light of a knowledge of 'how' to read it and what criteria to apply:

> *understanding is an event that happens within a relationship of vulnerability to the text* ... it arises out of a fusion of the contexts of both interpreter and text in the one fluid medium of an effective tradition ... when I set out to understand an author's [pupils'] text, I do not have to hand any method that will guarantee my success; and ... the author was similarly exposed when he set out to write it.[2] (my emphasis)

Since this young writer could not draw on any method of poetry writing which would guarantee in advance that what she wrote would be a successful poem, the teacher as reader is in a similarly vulnerable position in trying to understand it. If the writer writes the poem by submitting to a process over which she does not have fully conscious control, the reader can only begin to understand the poem by entering a similar state of vulnerability in trying to understand it. To begin reading a pupil's work by submitting oneself in this way is to alter the more usual set of power relations within which the reading of pupil's work normally takes place. It may be one of the reasons why students are not asked to write poetry as part of a state exam, and as such reflects the position of poetry not just outside the current of normal life, but outside normal assessment structures as well, a position of what might be called privileged 'exteriority'.

To place oneself as close reader, in a position of vulnerability without prescribed assessment criteria, in relation to this poem makes one come empty handed and therefore freer to 'pick up' the sense of resistance in the poem. The sense of difficulty for the writer in paying her poem the necessary attention is an understanding that is not external to the text, but, as will be seen, is close to the heart of the matter of the poem itself and to the process of assisting children in their writing. Understanding children's texts is a two-sided coin, one side of which is close reading, the other side being – especially for the inexperienced or uncertain teacher – close-writing-of that reading. In this instance, it was only through *writing about* Bríd's poem that the teacher came closer to understanding its internal dynamics.

Bríd's poem had arisen out of a unit of local history involving an exploration of the monuments, gravestones, place names and town lands of the locality, together with a rough census of the population, through which exploration children could be expected to 'acquire knowledge' of the place in which they lived. As has already been said, on first reading this poem seemed weightless and unremarkable. On closer reading and writing about the poem, its opening question hinted at a struggle in the mind of the writer to commit herself to believing in her local community being worth writing about. At the sub-textual level, it points to a struggle to commit her energy to the task, almost a 'would you' – that is, the audience, the teacher – 'write this poem if you had the choice?' Behind this opening lies another very important question about the nature of power relations in the classroom (e.g. who should have the authority to ask who to do what?) and the role of art (poetry in this particular instance) in the midst of those power relations (e.g. who or when can one legitimately refuse to even *try* to write poetry?) But one of the best ways to explore such questions is to stick closely to the text itself. Bríd's doubt about her local community having anything to recommend itself or mark its significance may have echoed the community's shallow faith in itself as anything special. Her doubt may also reflect the writer's shallow faith in her own ability to be a 'poet' (with all the rarity that that term often carries) or to write a poem that would 'turn out' to be anything special. It may reflect at a deeper level a scepticism in relation to poetry, a reluctance to 'do poetry' (a reluctance to which I was no stranger). Given the highly competitive nature of much in education, it is natural for children who don't 'win' poetry competitions, Young Scientist competitions, or any of the host of other competitions that promulgate themselves week in and week out, through primary schools, to believe that they are nothing special. It is extremely doubtful that Bríd's poem, had it been entered in a poetry competition, would have won, yet as will become clear, it is indeed a very special piece of writing. The area Bríd had written about was at the time (late eighties/early nineties) best known in the context of a television advertisement, spoken by a flat-accented, wellied, peak-capped farmer as being 'only an "ow-er" from

Dublin'. Only its relative distance from the country's capital city gave this writer's community any significance, analogous, perhaps, to the fact that the only significance many adults give to children's poetry is its relative closeness to 'the adult thing', not – as this poem in hindsight will show – for expressing an accurate view of children's reality. Her poetic diffidence may have echoed that of her community, which in turn echoed some rather negative national feeling, expressed in collective self-accusations that the country's politicians were going cap-in-hand to the European Community to look for all the structural funding they could get for this small country existing on Europe's periphery – only an hour or two from Brussels. Of course it would be absurd to suggest that these latter levels of significance existed in the conscious mind of the writer as she wrote her poem, but they are testimony to the nature of one of the 'gifts' of poetry rather than deliberate 'craft', in this particular instance that, in the process of making a poem, it may acquire resonances and meanings not initially part of the intention of the writer at all, a gift which Heaney compared to that of the diviner or dowser – something that could not be learned or acquired because it is 'a gift for being in touch with what is there, hidden and real, a gift for mediating between the latent resource and the community that wants it current and released'.[3]

At the level of hermeneutics, these resonances and meanings, not initially part of the intention of the writer at all, are testimony to the contribution the reader may bring to the potential meaning of the text too. They were not part of the initial intention of the reader either, but were generated out of her response to the text and 'brought to life' in language – the medium in which the reader and writer meet. It is through being active in language that text and interpreter enter a kind of conversation with each other, a conversation that is not a description, each of the other, but a game or play in which the participants – both text and reader – surrender to the primacy of the conversation, in which understanding, if it happens, happens *as a natural event*. The nature of this conversation, and indeed the nature of the *written conversation* between the poem in question and its reader, exemplifies 'good conversation' since:

> The whole point of conversation is that I both allow some play to my own thinking and, in doing so, expose it to the counterweight of the other's contribution, which may confirm me in it or force me to amend or abandon it ... we need to see that the meaning of the text has its *being* in the conversations in which it is brought into partnership.[4]

The significance of this kind of conversation for genuine education and critically for religious education cannot be underestimated. The classroom is at it most educational when it operates as a site in which such conversation is hosted by the teacher. In such situations, conversation *is* play and *as* play is beyond the control of any one of its participants, the game is on, the game that is language is being played and the participants have given themselves over to it, are taken up by it and the whole thing is 'an effort in extra time', time that is unforeseen and free, time that is surely in a religious sense Kingdom time. This is the epitome not only of education but of a religious education that is utterly Spirited. It has shaken off the technicist confines of specified outcomes and higher and lower order questions and answers because the outcome is pure gift, a kind of educational grace bestowed on those who took part, who gave themselves over to it, and for which they may say 'Thanks be to God'. It is learning that is blessing-in-return.

Close reading is essentially a process whereby the text and the teacher/reader are brought into genuine, close conversation. As close reader, it is the responsibility of the teacher/reader to offer the writer the insights she brings into conversation with it, so that the writer may develop an appreciation of, to paraphrase Patrick Kavanagh, the ways in which poetry 'must be allowed to surprise us'. In the discovery of deeper levels within it, the poem begins to 'come into its own being', to grow in significance at the level of task, and at the level of meaning in the poem itself, and encourages the writer's (and perhaps too, her community's) sense of identity and self-worth. All of these are what the writer had been struggling with (echoing the young apprentice-poet Muirgen's struggle on behalf of his community) and through the languaged processes of writing and close reading, experience and understanding are nourished. In this way the teacher has hopefully nourished the poem to 'quickening' in its writer so that it becomes, as Professor Cox puts it, more 'vigorous, committed, honest and interesting'.[5]

'There's the school there's the pub/There's the church and the youth club' suggests a bored eleven-year-old giving a perfunctory, polite tour of the locality to a visitor whose interest in the place seems unwarranted. The temptation of an arm's length reading of this poem would be to collude with the mood of the writer and move on to some other place, some other child's poem, more immediately interesting, more promising. In essence, the teacher/tourist has asked for a conducted tour of this child's locality and, within the power relations of the classroom, that request is being complied with. However, 'where there is no true kinship of interests, where power relations determine the conditions of meeting, linguistic exchange becomes a duel ... Children guard their preserve',[6] this poem seeks to comply with the teacher's 'invitation' to write and, at the same time, to say as little as possible. But however little is being said, much is meant! The writer has offered a tour of the institutional locality. The church, the pub, the school and the youth club are the cornerstones of every ordinary rural parish. Their ordinariness is part of their being fundamental and vice versa. Description of them has no need to be elaborate. It is sufficient for the writer simply to state the fact of their being. The rhyming of 'pub' and 'club' establishes a pairing between these two over and against the other two which, then, by implication, also form a pair (indeed they look straight at each other from opposite sides of the road). The implications of the tensions inherent in their hidden relationship – as opposed to being out there in rhyme and sound – constitute a source of ongoing controversy in the State. Again, these are levels of significance that have not been consciously willed by the writer, but to point to them is to affirm the non-technical nature of poetry and to affirm it as 'gift' in the experience of the writer.

Life in this poem is seen in the context of the institutions within which it is lived, as opposed to the physical environment – nature and rural setting – which often 'grabs attention' as being more 'poetic'. The perception of this eleven-year-old, expressed via the poem, hints at a dawning consciousness of the social world and engagement with a critical process:

> As children, one of our tasks is to enter the symbolic order, to acknowledge it and position ourselves in it so that we can speak as members of a culture – if we fail the result is psychosis.[7]

It may be this not-yet-fully-developed understanding which has cast the poem between the two worlds that constitute it – the institutional and the individual.

And then there's Richard/Stabannon's main man/Who'll hold his head high/Just to show that he can. The writer's presentation of Richard, the individual, is immediately energetic, rhythmic, rhyming, confident and definite. It contrasts not only the individual with the institution, but interest with boredom, energy with apathy, individual identity with institutional anonymity. Richard is a self-declaration of individual freedom (an interesting symbol in this instance, given the power relations within which the poem is written; perhaps Richard represents the writer's would-be challenge to the teacher and the task) as against collective dependence. Perhaps it is Richard, perhaps it is the individual, perhaps it is freedom, perhaps it is just 'being oneself' which need no justification as to why these are what they are, other than childhood's direct answer to every why –'Just!' Richard stands as a four-line structure, four-square over and against the basic institutions of rural living, head and shoulders above the rest of the community, a position underlined by the phrase 'Stabannon's main man'. Richard is obvious; Richard is a 'show'; Richard is celebration of the individual as challenge to the institutional. Confirmation of this interpretation and of poetry's way of operating below conscious levels of thought and feeling may be found in a fact probably not known to the young writer, i.e. that Richard's name derives from the Germanic elements *'ric'* meaning power, rule, and *'hard'*, meaning brave, strong.

The poem in its energy, its mood, its pattern, seems cyclical; it ends as it began with the question: 'Would you live in Stabannon/if you had the choice?' But the question with which the writer began is not the same as the one with which she ends because the actual writing of the poem has altered it. It is as though in her repetition, the writer holds the question of the creative tension between the individual and the institution in society – a much more creative act than simply giving one or other of them 'the last word' in the last line. The repetition of 'you' in the final question (underscored by the absence anywhere in the poem of 'me' or 'I', an indication of the extent to which the author wishes to 'guard her preserve' as Steiner said) is like an insistent finger pointing at the reader/teacher, a direct challenge to choose which, if any, Stabannon to live in. It is as though the poem answers an injunction, 'Write a poem about your locality', with another injunction 'You choose'. Children as a sub-cultural group have little or no choice as to where they live; adults may assume that they, as adults, do have a choice. The question of choice, and in relation to what, where and whom, are central to this poem, as indeed they are to life itself. In this way the poem is a kind of metaphor for the power struggle between childhood and adulthood, between authority and dependence, between individuality and collectivity, between dominant culture and sub-culture.

This then is a reluctant writer's first (and probably, in her estimation, last) draft of a poem. It leads into another part of the writing process, to what Professor Cox and also the Southern curriculum refer to as 'drafting, editing and refining', in which children are given opportunities to 're-read their writing as if they were in the intended reader's place, and to revise, redraft and proof-read their work with the reader in mind'.[8]

For the writer, the process of drafting is about honing, refining, shaping, making and remaking changes, both compositional and secretarial, as one writes, as well as in the retrospective light of the conversation between the teacher/reader, the writer and the text. The scope of this conversation, which has been explored in the context of close reading of Bríd's poem, is extended in the drafting process; it is as though the teacher has arrived at a point where she can say, 'I am beginning to understand what you are trying to express; now, how can I offer you *real* and *practical* help in expressing it?' It is important to note, however, that this understanding is not a once-off appropriation of 'the meaning' of the poem; it is an ongoing process of dialogue with the developing text and its developing writer by the developing teacher exemplifying a conversational process:

> ... conversation is not something that happens *after* I have first understood the text – when secure in my understanding of it, I then confront it with my own thought. Rather, my own thought has been in a kind of inter-play with it all along, and only within this inter-play do I come to understand it at all.[9]

The richer the quality of conversation the emerging writing participates in, the deeper the potential learning. Following on his comment on close reading James Britton points to the explicit nature of reader-help:

> Children value perceptive comments, responses and questions on their writing, but they quickly see through perfunctory approval and generalised faint praise. And it is worth remembering that for very many children, for very many years, their teachers are the only readers of the bulk of their work.[10]

Such explicitness is in sharp contrast to the attitude that generated much of the suspicion highlighted in *The Verbal Arts Manifesto*, in which many teachers were suspicious of 'creative writing' as self-indulgent and undisciplined.

> One of the problems ... was that progression was often not planned for, the assumption being that pupils would make progress simply by repeating poetry writing. This is not necessarily the case, however, particularly for reluctant writers who feel little more than frustration when they are confronted

> with the demands to write yet another poem, with little indication from the teacher about how to do it better, apart from the encouraging comment, 'Quite good', 'Fair', 'Keep trying', hurriedly written at the bottom. Assessment is difficult where poetry is concerned ... How then are teachers to be encouraging and at the same time ensure that their apprentices learn from one attempt to another?[11]

What is interesting is that the pupil and her teacher face the same problem: the writer/pupil tries to be accurately expressive in her writing and the teacher must also try to be equally accurate and precise in her comments, observations and insights into that writing, and must seek to communicate them in a way that the pupil can understand and therefore transfer (as and when she chooses) into the writing itself. Of critical importance, if this process is to be effective, will be that which Cox pointed to at the beginning of this chapter, i.e. the teacher's *experience* of the process of writing developed from knowledge and understanding of the practice of real writers, *including herself*. Belonging as it does to 'praxis/phronesis', poetry writing is an activity in which knowledge is experiential, gained *within* the writing process, as one tries it out oneself and close-watches established writers doing so too, and not from some vantage point outside the act of writing. The teacher who would teach children about writing poetry will have significant experience to draw on if she is also *a practising writer*, regardless, for the moment, of how successful or otherwise she is, and taking comfort in her nervousness about calling herself a 'writer', or even worse, a poet, from the fact that, as Brendan Kennelly has said, it matters less who writes the poems than that the poems gets written. The overall thrust of the drafting process is to increase precision and accuracy so that the eventual finished poem expresses the particularity or the peculiar 'thisness' of its subject, e.g. Ted Hughes' crowiness of the crow; in other words the uniqueness and precision with which poetry re-imagines experience into words.[12]

The act of writing and the action of a poetic education actively fosters the expression of 'thisness', of the unique essence, the truth, of a person or an experience. Such an education is intimate with the essential action at the heart of poetic language – the search for the right words at the right moment, whether that search comes up trumps or not. Such an education nourishes people who are not satisfied just to categorise experience according to general classification, or know the world objectively, as our study of Stabannon via census, annotation, description, etc. would do. Such an education seeks to nourish its participants poetically so that their speaking is at the same time an action to transform existence into something known intimately and wisely, rather than objectively, because that is how, through poetry, it has been experienced. An education that is intimate with the poetic seeks not just to engage with the world but to make some meaning out of the experience of engaging.

An example of teaching and learning that is intimate with the poetic is offered in the next poem which is not only of an attempt to make something of the experience of looking at some wildflowers but of the importance of the teacher having *real* experience of the impulse and the carrying through of the impulse to *make in writing* something of what she herself sees and to offer it to her students as an example of how they too might proceed. The poem's writer was invited to become involved with another class's environmental studies project exploring the effects of a new motorway on the wildlife of the parish. The class's interest in the teacher's help was based on the fact that she had an interest in photography; they felt they needed pictures from the locality to help illustrate their project, pictures of, among other things, local flora and fauna. Although this was not the kind of photography this teacher usually engaged in, it forced her to look at wild flowers 'close up', in a way and with a concentration she had never previously regarded them. Photography and poetry have much in common: they are both arts concerned with 'exposing the image'. As the photographer looked through her lens, she was struck by the strength of colour and geometric character of the common dandelion as she tried to 'capture' it from this angle and that angle. Her subsequent poem was an attempt to capture this same colour and character in words, to 'make something' of what she had seen. Just as the photographer runs a conversation in her head as she shoots, about shutter speeds, apertures, fields of focus, backgrounds etc., so the writer in this poem (mindful of her role as teacher) holds a conversation with the process of writing as she writes. She commits this conversation to paper so that students may see that she, like many poets, bears witness to the through-other logic of the writing process.

Wild Life of the Dandelion *(Taraxacum Dens-leonis)*

The writer's experience of the unique 'character' of the dandelion is what is at stake in this poem. It is the flower's essential character that slips the knot of the title's attempt to identify it, to 'call it' as it were, by its botanical categorisation. Education may legitimately seek to help pupils to 'know' the contours of the world around them according to categories and pre-established definitions but an education that is intimate with the poetic will seek to help them to register in words their experience of that world in all its uniqueness, in its true 'character'. Just as through her study of the facts and figures of the locality Bríd came to know her parish in a dispassionate geo-historical sense, her poem sponsored a more intimate knowing, a knowing of the

Taraxacum Deus Leonis

Dandelion
punky fellow
mad died hair –
electric yellow.
Dandelion
A Simpson sprat
Bart of the spring fields,
Hedgerow brat.
Dandelion
best beware
Puff, puff, puff...
Goodbye hair!
"So who cares",
says Bart-de-lion
"Homer head
Suits me fine"
D'oh!

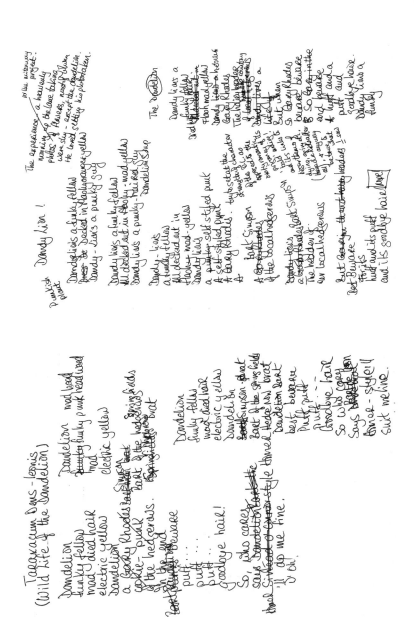

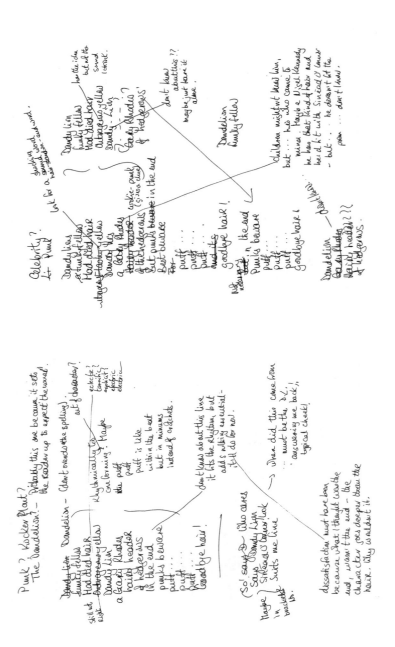

'character' of the parish that is not completely separable from the person or character that Bríd herself is. The process of writing her poem actualised both these characters more fully, brought them both to greater fullness of life. But coming to fullness of life is not a process over which one can, as it were, stand back and spectate, exercise remote control. Similarly a poem is a happening, not a predictable or guaranteeable outcome. The writing of a poem is never therefore the result of an applied methodology. In this way every new attempt at a poem is, for its writer and its teacher, an entering into darkness. It is language searching the pockets of experience, a searching in which fingers become eyes-out-on-sticks, antennae scanning the darkness. It is a process that must trust in language, in memory, experience and the resourcefulness of relevant skills honed during other entries into other darknesses, other rummagings in other pockets. Writing each new poem and nourishing and fostering the writing of each new poem will always involve uncertainty, contingency and, because of these, vulnerability; it can never 'take shelter from the darkness' as Muirgen's young companion did; it will always have a strong element of unpredictability and ad-hocness. But it is not completely hazardous. It is not a boat without a rudder, though the rudder is made of language and the skills needed to steer or negotiate are linguistic. And the teacher needs to have the balance and skills to 'teach from the boat'. Neither is the 'fully alive' religion lesson the result of a methodology; it too must go deeper into knowing than surface fact and dogma; it too seeks to actualise coming to greater fullness of life; it too is a searching in experience's dark pockets that promise their share of gift, of blessing in return for pushing out from the shore, for trusting beyond methodology. The teacher who has faith in the poetic or faith in the Word repeatedly made flesh knows that true religious education puts its trust in language as the fluid in which understanding, interpretation, cumulative correction and refinement, and conversation, is conducted. The ebb and flow of language's conversational tides are the primary processes in education's oral tradition. The challenge to the teacher today is to keep imaginative faith in the capacity of education suffused with poetry and its writing process to ride the winds, waves and currents of life's ceaseless motion.

Returning to Bríd's poem, conversation between the teacher and the writer suggested that a second draft of this poem might try to further particularise Richard against the background of where he lives by 'heavy-outlining him' or 'colouring him in a bit' and adding specific detail to his presentation:

> **Would you live in Stabannon if you had the choice?**
> There's the school for the children
> There's the pub for the men
> There's the church for the women
> There's the youth-club for in-between.
> Richard doesn't fit anywhere there
> He just walks the roads, he doesn't care.
> Richard is Stabannon's main man
> Who'll hold his head high just to show that he can.
> He'll smoke in your face
> Flick his ash with such grace
> Smile all down the aisle from Communion.
> Would you live in Stabannon
> If you had the choice?

Draft two is significantly more detailed than the first. Institutional images have been coloured in with their membership but are still general and non-personalised. The image of Richard has been highlighted and coloured in with rhyme and movement and action and emotion. One senses in the broad-vowelled rhyming of 'aisle' and 'smile' an immense ear-to-ear grin; a smile that is too broad to be devious, yet lets the reader see the twinkle or 'lightness' in the eye, perhaps reflecting a lightness in the soul. Richard is suggestively 'simple', yet subconsciously a very complex archetypal 'character' who inhabits the soul of many a rural Irish community. He has within him something of the 'Bird' in John B. Keane's *The Field*, or Patrick Kavanagh's 'Green Fool'. The challenge of his smoke-in-your-face, allied with the graceful flick of politically and socially incorrect cigarette ash, gesture at a connoisseurship, a gift for deeply inhaling one's mortality and puffing it nonchalantly in the community's face (and in the face of its immortal God/s). The full significance of 'Communion' may not be within the writer's grasp but the keenness of the detail with which she depicts Richard suggests that she knows him as well as Brendan Kennelly knew his three-year-old. She balances him delicately in a smile – without which his challenge to her and her community's understanding of their identity might not be so 'poetic'. The continuing conversation between teacher and writer resulted in the discarding of 'Richard doesn't fit ... he doesn't care', since they seemed to speak *for* Richard instead of letting Richard, through his actions, speak for himself. They robbed the poem of some of its creative tension by over-explaining, thereby compromising the character of Richard. Richard is not the kind of character anyone could reliably 'speak for' since one never knows what he is likely to come out with. It was also decided that the third draft might accentuate Richard further, stress his individuality by using his name instead of 'He'. It was hoped that this repetition, this *sounding* of Richard, might almost become – in terms of the aural dimension of the poem – a vocal 'nuisance', but a valuable insistence on his individuality and freedom to be 'who' he is. Such a hope would have to be vindicated or negated by speaking the poem; literally 'sounding it out' to see whether or not it worked.

It was decided that these changes should stay and that the poem was now 'finished' and only needed a title to be complete. Finding a title for a poem is not always easy and the learning inherent in naming one's poem should not be underestimated. In naming her poem the writer comes to a total sense of the poem as a finished work, echoing that 'right' naming is 'the first foundation/For telling truth'.[13] In this case the writer – perhaps caught in the midst of those tensions she manages so successfully in the poem – hesitates between the titles 'Richard', 'Stabannon' and 'Choices'. The teacher suggested 'Communion', since this seemed capable of holding nuances of all three, but later withdrew the suggestion as inappropriate adult sophistication or just 'smartness'. Ironically, the title eventually arrived at was 'You Choose', which of course suits the poem perfectly. Just as the title of a poem is important, so also is the act of signing one's name to the poem one has made. The stamp of this personal hallmark is important in developing the writer's psychological sense of self as a writer. Such a sense may be well-rounded in the mature writer, but in the 'shy soul' it must be nourished and affirmed, both in the writing and speaking of one's poem and in the signing of one's name to identify oneself as 'poet' or 'file', with a growing sense of the truth in that naming too.

Some critics have argued that this pupil's poem in its 'finished' form is less suggestive, more 'obvious' than in its original first draft. This is a valid criticism and, like the painting poem earlier, it raises two important questions – when is a poem finished i.e. when do I as writer stop writing; and the counterpart of that question for the teacher – when should I stop teaching? In fact, should the teacher ever do anything to alter children's writing; should it not be taken as given? There are no easy answers, no guaranteed methods for deciding when or even if a poem should be 'worked with'. It is not always easy to decide when a poem is 'finished'. Every artist knows that at a certain point one must 'let go' and every teacher has seen the painting that went too far and ends up as a sodden hole in the middle of the page. The relationship between product and process is a complex one. Perhaps Bríd's poem was finished after her first draft, perhaps the 'truth' of what she had to say was there, full stop. Perhaps she had said all that was to be said and the rest was 'not her business'. To the extent that poetry is a craft, then it can be taught/learned – as Yeats said, a trade – and it can practice singing what is well made. To the extent that it is gift it cannot be taught and must be courted. But even as gift, poetry requires recognition and appreciation and has – at least initially – to be fostered as also does the gift of teaching. The process of fostering – in both the teacher and the pupil – an appreciation of poetry involves the development of a language in which to hold conversation about it, in which to relate to it. Much of the drafting process is the holding of just such a conversation. Ultimately, with regard to whether Bríd's poem is more or less poetic in its first or last draft – 'You Choose'.

What has been made more explicit here, in a poem that was chosen for its 'seeming lack of poesy', is the role of close reading and drafting in learning to be a writer and learning to be a teacher of writing. It is a process of questioning, shaping, redefining, judging. It is an experience for the teacher of nourishing in the tongue, mind, voice, eye and ear of the young writer as well as in herself a process akin to the game of marbles with its

> ... anglings, aimings, feints and squints
> You were allowed before you'd shoot, all those
>
> Hunkerings, tensings, pressures of the thumb,
> Test-outs and pull backs, re-envisagings ...[14]

before the last full stop. The wider educational role of what is being practised and learnt through drafting and redrafting is the internality of critical judgement to the artistic activity itself.[15]

And further out, what is being practised and learnt is the internality of critical judgement to the living of life, moment by moment, day by day and in situations of varying power-relations. It is the process through which and only *through* which the artist – in this case the child as writer, and the other side of that coin, the teacher as 'nourisher' or 'fosterer'– learns how to:

> tell whether he is pursuing it [the writing or nourishing] successfully or unsuccessfully ... it is possible for him to say, 'I am not satisfied with that line; let us try it this way ... and this way ... and this way ... there! That will do' ... The watching of his own work with a vigilant and discriminating eye, which decides at every moment of the process whether it is being successful or not, is not a critical activity subsequent to and reflective upon, the artistic work, it is an integral part of that work itself ... In point of fact, what a student learns in art-school is ... to watch himself painting.[16]

What a child learns gradually is not only to write but to watch herself writing, just as what the teacher learns is not only how to teach but to watch herself teaching. The kind of understanding generated by this close-reading-drafting-close re-reading re-drafting process is of the essence of the to-and-fro-ness of all genuine understanding. It is valid of course to question the degree of consciousness with which children should/do write and it may be argued that with regard to consciousness and the writing process, 'less is more'. But children's capacity for critical thinking or adjudication of their work as it 'makes its way onto the page' may be greater than they are often given credit for. For example:

My Dog
I got a dog!
I called him Chancer!
I only had him three weeks!
He got sick!
He died!
(Donal, First Class/P.3)

When asked about his unusual use of exclamation marks – which nuance the writing significantly – Donal explained that because everybody was using full stops he was fed up with them! His choice was a very deliberate and conscious one in accordance with a definite criteria which, although he may not have articulated to himself at the time, he was nevertheless able to articulate.

To return to Bríd's poem again, another truth of this poem is that the young poet speaks a truth of her local community and her poem is, therefore, an actualisation of conscience:

Conscience demands that we speak out what we all know together because we mustn't suppress it ... by telling his own secrets the writer tells the secrets of the community. Their marginalised self, the secret self, somehow is pacified and they feel more at ease. I think if things are brought out into the open without aggression, as image rather than accusation, then things are helped along. I think the writer has to invent a vicarious examination for other people.[17]

This suggestion keeps company with a spirit of community that challenges the urge towards individualism and self-sufficiency. A practice such as writing is vulnerable and contingent precisely because, even if the poet sits at a desk in a study all by him or herself, it is *not* a solitary function; it is dependent on language and language is a shared 'thing' within human living. Language is not something a poet acts on, but rather acts *within*. Therefore, engaging with language as writing does challenges individualism and its offspring, competitiveness. One's poetry is not the result of individual skill or even inspiration acting upon a grammar and vocabulary (even though these are obviously vital). Writers are a community '... collective. Writers are a system of energy of some sort. They're an ecology ... In the end, we poets are not in competition, we're all delivering the goods'.[18]

The role of the teacher in relation to poetry in education is not therefore to act on either language or the pupil and shape him or her into a poet. It is to recognise the limits of what can be taught and give credit to the potential of fostering, in whatever way the teacher can, a school community in which the poet is 'spoken' alive and well. People 'become poets or painters or musicians not by some process of development from within ... but by living in a society where these languages are current'.[19] Similarly people become 'religious' or 'prophetic' by living in a society in which these languages are current, and are fostered, nourished and developed in a religious education alive to the nature of language and particularly the poetic. In short the teacher has to imitate the digger and shovel and clear out whatever staunches the flow of the poetic through the life of the school community.

Notes

1. *Cox on Cox,* p. 149.
2. *Back to the Rough Ground,* p. 116.
3. *Preoccupations,* pp. 47–8.
4. *Back to the Rough Ground,* p. 117.
5. *The Cox Report,* Chapter 10:19, p. 48.
6. *After Babel,* p. 7.
7. Cameron, D., *Feminism and Linguistic Theory,* London, Macmillan, 1992, 2nd edn, p. 163.
8. *Primary School Curriculum,* Chapter 10:33, p. 52.
9. *Back to the Rough Ground,* p. 84.
10. *The Cox Report,* 10.43, pp. 53–4.
11. *Things Made and Things Said,* p. 68.
12. Ibid., p. 60. ' ... the degree of precision and accuracy which it [poetry] achieves in remaking experience in all its individuality: its colour, shape and sound, together with the emotions and feelings which it generates.'
13. Heaney, *An Open Letter,* Field Day Theatre Company, 1983.
14. *Seeing Things,* p. 57.
15. *Back to the Rough Ground,* p. 73.
16. Ibid., p. 74.
17. *Things Made and Things Said,* p. 19.
18. Seamus Heaney, *Irish Times,* Saturday, 30 October 1999.
19. *Back to the Rough Ground,* p. 82.

8 Craft and Gift

Thus far this book has tried to specify the nature of the writing process and its significance as a model of education intimately concerned with language, learning, understanding and experience. Returning to the beginning, to chapter four's question 'Where does poetry come from?' it is not just experience that the children writing that poem must search through; more accurately, it is experience *remembered*. Memory searching is another micro-process within poetry writing. Memory though is not just a warehouse in which 'stuff' is stored and pulled out into use as and when required. It is potentially a recycling plant. Great poets are those whose processing capacity is such that it can recycle not only their individual experience but collective experience also such as was evident earlier in the link between Heaney's 'orphaned memory' and the poets of Ireland's 'memory orphaned'. Those links are an indication of how poets on behalf of society searched memory, re-processing experience and ultimately recycling or renewing that society's identity and with it, I suggest, education's identity. This is a process that is ongoing and life-long.

A key overlap of the searching of memory in the process of writing is the searching for image. Searching for images is another micro-process within poetry writing. It is as though language and experience seek each other through the medium of the image – aural or visual. The process of 'using your imagination' becomes more accurately a process of paying particular attention. It is a process of refining the image from its initial blurred appearance, through a vague series of hunches, intuitions, synchronicities or accidents until, in time, it becomes identifiable. In 'Sticky Poetry', it is the search-through-memory of other searches that provides the images or 'sharpened vision' of the complex nature of poetry. Enabling and encouraging pupils to search for and learn how to hone images, that is, to take their first blurred impressions and pare the crude image until it is 'Refined beyond the dross into sheer image',[1] is a process in which, as a writer herself, with knowledge of the practices of other writers, the teacher will know instinctively how to assist her pupils. As a writer herself she will know how and when to 'grip expectant wrists', how to 'hunt the pluck' and how to recognise when the 'hazel has stirred' – and equally importantly, when it has not.[2] Sometimes this can be a matter of picking up on what the Kingman Report suggested earlier: feeding or nourishing children who are working with a particular subject, with the images of great poets on that same subject, or at a wider level, steeping them, like peas, in the poetry and way-with-image of such as Ted Hughes in, for example, 'The Warm and the Cold':

> ... the carp in its depth
> Like a planet in its heaven.
> And the badger in its bedding
> Like a loaf in the oven.
> And the butterfly in its mummy
> Like a viol in its case.
> And the owl in its feathers
> Like a doll in its lace ...
>
> ... the trout in its hole
> Like a chuckle in a sleeper

The hare stares down the highway
Like a root going deeper.
The snail is dry in the outhouse
Like a seed in a sunflower.
The owl is pale on the gatepost
Like a clock on its tower ...

... the cod in the tide-rip
Like a key in a purse.
The deer are on the bare blown hill
Like smiles on a nurse.
The flies are behind the plaster
Like the lost score of a jig.
Sparrows are in the ivy clump
Like money in a pig ...[3]

Or savouring herself the images of such poets as Norman McCaig, *lightening and straw* images that have the sharpness of a blade of seemingly innocent grass. It is not always an easy task, given the conceptual, analytical urges of our scientific, utilitarian and increasingly jargon-speaking educational culture, to help children to search for fresh images. This is especially true in those times when, as the teacher will know from her experience, one must accept one's lack of control of the writing process and simply have the patience to wait for an image to approach or just to turn up. At other times, it will be a process of enticing images, like strategically opening a window and door in one's mind, in the knowledge that they will cause a 'mental draught', sucking images in so that hopefully one's poetic instinct can leap to catch one as one would leap to catch a door that is about to slam. The process of looking or searching for image and metaphor implies that they have a strong element of hiddenness – hidden meaning, hidden reality or hidden agenda. But it is this very *hidden* element that allows the image to be fresh, accurate, explicit, to surprise, to evoke in the reader that spontaneous 'Ah Yes!' in response to it. In order to find out whether or not an image is fresh, children must test it out by squeezing it like a loaf on the corner-shop shelf. They must learn to interrogate it, asking specific questions of it, so that it is particularised in their own individual experience. Ted Hughes offers advice in this regard when he suggests that the writer

> ... look at it, listen to it, turn yourself into it ... keep your eyes, your ears, your nose, your taste, your touch, your whole being on the thing you are turning into words.[4]

The first images children offer for an emotion or an event are often couched in abstract propositions:

> Boring is when you're fed up.
> Boring is when you've nothing to do.
> Boring is when you've no one to play with.

But here are more specific, more sharply pin-pointed images of boredom:

> Boring is the tin of biscuits when the fancy ones are all gone.
> Boring is when the ball has a dead bounce 'cos it's bust.
> Boring is Sunday afternoon when grown-ups sleep behind the papers.
> Boring is when the fizz is all out of the Coke.
> Boring is Daniel O'Donnell on Top of the Pops.

Children find it easier to identify fresh images if they are wrapped in personally experienced actuality, for example, in these images of Spring:

Spring is
- Taking off your shoes and socks to race in the grass
- Smelling the newly cut lawn
- Tying your jumper round your waist 'cos you're too warm
- White legs and arms 'cos the jumpers are off
- Not many swans left on the bog
- The feeling just to go for a walk
- First time you take your bike instead of the school bus
- Salad instead of hot dinner
- Not noticing the fire's out.

As opposed to:

Spring is
- snowdrops and daffodils
- animals come out of hibernation
- leaves come on the trees
- the birds sing
- the lambs play in the fields.

In the first set of images, the language is exact because it is directly linked to the experiences of the class and reflects their ability to seduce from memory accurate images that express them. In the second, on the other hand, the images may of course be real, but are more like the received images in which Spring is stereotyped or clichéd. The role of the teacher, as well as observing the difference in the kinds of images offered, is, in the interests of effective teaching and learning, to wonder why this difference occurs in the first place. Close observation of the images in question suggests that those latter stereotypical images appear to be almost a *classification* of Spring as though it were a 'species' of 'season', to be 'labelled, identified' and hence objectively or scientifically known. The criteria according to which it is being classified seems to be 'what happens in Spring, relative to what happens in other seasons'. The kind of knowledge that 'springs' to mind for these children is the scientific knowledge of the nature study lesson. The first set of images, on the other hand, do not generalise, but particularise Spring; the knowledge being called on is experiential, and in the process of its being recalled, Spring is rendered 'more intimately knowable'. If these observations are accurate, then one may place one's understanding of the process of formulating these different types of images against the background of

> Aristotle's concern to establish the lineaments of a new, well-founded *episteme*, based on strict classification according to genus and species, and governed by explicitly formulated logical procedures.[5]

Part of what these children may be experiencing (though not consciously) is the problem of Aristotle's success in bending language to support a 'logic of definition' over and against the

> 'living, metaphoric nature of language' ... whose continual improvisation within the 'free universality of language' [allows that] what emerges is a new, more specific word-formation which does more justice to the particular features of the subject matter.[6]

Teaching that seeks to assist pupils in moving from stereotypical or generalised images to particular, fresh images is engaged in a very fundamental educational struggle. It seeks to redress a linguistic imbalance aggravated by a technical, rational mode of linguistic definition. In doing so the inherent metaphoric nature of language may be free to provide children with the subsoil of thought in which images and words begin to articulate thoughts, concepts and other images adequate to their aspirations and desperations.

Having searched and found, if not what they were searching for, at least enough image to be going on with for the moment, children can begin to play and enter into that first sense of crafting words, working with 'rhythms and noises', a 'dabbling', an 'arranging', a 'game', a 'word-play', in 'trial-pieces' such as:

Sum Master!
Sumhow
Sumtime
Sum where
Sum one or
Sumthing
Will tell the master to
Sum-up!
(But not me)
(3rd/4th class/P.4/5)

Poor Me
Poor me
Poor me
It's always the same
I wanted it fancy
It ended up plain.

Poor me
Poor me
It's terribly sad
For when I'm without it
It drives me quite mad!
(Bríd, 5th class/P.6)

The Argos Catalogue
Imagine an Argos Catalogue
Of poems and rhymes
All for something pounds
Ninety-nine!
(A poetic bargain)
(Ciara, 6th class)

No Idea
My mind is
A remote control
Without a battery,
When it comes to poetry.
(Wayne, 5th class/P.7)

Nice One
There are all kinds of pets
Pet dogs
Pet cats
Pet rabbits
Pet mice.

There are all kinds
Of words
Bad words
Good words
Big words
Small words
I have a pet word.

She is 'Nice'.
Nice'n easy
Nice'n comfortable
Nice'n kind
Nice'n warm.

Most people don't like Nice.
They say she is
Too plain
Too common
Too much
But I think Nice
She's just Gorgeous.
(Cathy, 5th class)

Set Exercise
... eventually you choose

A pile of stones discarded
by an entrance gate
like leftovers scraped
to the side of a plate

For a solid hour your gaze
searched them like those ants
in a frantic hunt
for some significance

Sixty dry-cracked, sun-baked minutes
staring blind at stones ...
that's enough of that then
give it up,
go home

Stood up, turned to go
took a step,
stopped –
behind your back a deafening silence
suddenly opened up

Whirled around
held your breath
listening hard heard
a stubborn stone rebuttal
word upon word

stone me, no need to be, looked at wondered about
understood written about talked about fed put to bed
no need to speak to do to think to imagine to sleep to
dream to be or not to be to diet no striving no craving
no effort no like no dislike no envy no restlessness no
resentment no ambition possessing a history but no
need to recall it possessing a future but no need to
worry about it no need of darkness or light no need of
air of people of a pension of good luck of education
dry but never thirsty rained on but never soaked
crawled over poked under turned over stared at
trampled on frosted over sun-baked cut built blown
up no need no matter each an original perfect
individual stone of its own

Lot's wife then
answer me this:
being turned to stone –
was it blight or bliss?

These attempts at poetry are, for the children and teacher
involved, what those 'little inept designs in imitation of the
master's fluent interlacing patterns, heavy-handed clues to the
whole craft'[7] were to the early Heaney. They are a conscious
savouring of the process of writing as well as the delight in
words themselves; they celebrate the craft of making as well
as the gift of being able to say something 'true'. They
exemplify the process that will 'enable pupils to exercise more
conscious and critical control over the writing process'.[8]

While it is undoubtedly true that 'a poet could have a real technique and a wobbly craft ... but more often it is a case of a sure enough craft and a failure of technique',[9] nevertheless, the 'mix' of craft to gift is rarely ever even. And whereas it is true that, as Bullock has already said, 'Poetry works best when it is wanted', one cannot simply wait around in the classroom in anticipation of 'the moment'; school is a place in which the fostering of skills in anticipation of the bigger event is a legitimate task. In 'Poem Switch', for example, the method or craft being practised is to take an event – the writing of a poem – explore it in terms of its contents, concentrate on what is foremost in that event – the emotion of frustration at how difficult or awkward it is to 'get into it' – and search the memory for images of other experiences that have also been frustrating:

> It's like when you're in bed and you waken because you have to go to the toilet and it's dark and you don't know where you are and you're trying to find the light switch and you know it's there but still, you can't find it and you have to grope around in the dark. (Grace)

The skills needed at this point are those a child uses in mixing colours while painting. Take some of the words and phrases from the image of searching in the dark for the light switch and mix them in with the words needed to describe the writing of a poem; for example, instead of a light switch, make it a poem switch; instead of trying to see, make it trying to write; instead of you being in the darkness, the darkness is inside you – in your head. The result is:

Poem Switch
I grope for a poem switch
In my head
But it's all dark in there

I can't find the light
To write.
(Grace, 6th class)

Ruth's poem below is a similar overlapping of two ideas –
the idea of building a poem and the idea of building a hut is
testimony to Eliot's contention that 'poetry is made with
words'. The words and images taken from the child's
recounting of her experience of actually building a hut out
of branches and things is superimposed on her experience of
writing a poem, which is more difficult to articulate.
Working with words and images in this way is like working
with one of those little mosaic-type puzzles in which one
slides the various squares over and back and up and down
to try to arrive at the completed picture, or the numbers in
the correct sequence. Here the writer is trying to arrive at
the best arrangement of the words – 'the best words in the
best order'. As part of this process, words such as 'ideas',
'words', 'poem' and so on are arranged in the physical
landscape of the poem among 'fields', 'branches', 'cows' etc.

Hideout
I live beside a
field of ideas.

I made a poem hut there
Out of words and branches and twigs.

There are cows wondering
In my field of ideas.

Cows knock
My poem hut down.

They think my field of ideas
Is theirs to eat.

Cows don't understand my poetry.

But even this example of poetry writing with a large degree of very deliberate craft displays the wisdom of not becoming too definitive about a poem's writing processes as opposed to its accident of birth. The accident in the case of Ruth's poem happened as a result of what can only be called 'poetic collusion' or, more accurately perhaps, 'collision' between elements of the kind of aural intelligence referred to earlier: sound and meaning. Ruth is a cheerfully polite little girl who makes every effort to speak 'properly'. To the teacher it seems that, as Ruth concentrated on writing the final draft of her poem in her very best writing she was also saying the poem to herself in her very best voice. The interconnectedness of what Heaney refers to when he says that 'a poetic voice is probably connected with the poet's natural voice, the voice that he hears as the ideal speaker of the lines he is making up'[10] resulted in a linguistic 'tweak' in Ruth's poem and she wrote 'wondering', instead of 'wandering'. It had the effect, however, of transforming a straightforward enough poem, owing more to hard graft than anything else, giving it 'a whole new quickened sense' of itself, because on close reading it became apparent that those dumb animals were bestowed with the *wonder* of huge eyes, like capital 'Ohs', gazing in amazement as they *wandered* through that field of ideas.

The meeting of voice and ear coinciding the 'a' and the 'o' are similar to the meeting between tooth and tongue in the first part of Tara's poem, 'Shaky Tooth':

> A shaky tooth
> And a pushy tongue
> Just can't leave
> Each other alone.

Although Tara went on to write another four lines to finish her poem, in essence these four lines are all that need to be said. They immediately strike a home run and in doing so mirror the deeper relationship between craft and gift in poetry; because in a very real sense, they craft and gift or *phronesis* and *techne* in poetry, 'can't leave each other alone'. Returning to a different but related image of language, that of the game used by Merleau-Ponty, the relationship between craft and gift in poetry reaches its most artistic when the two meet each other, centre of gravity to centre of gravity, as in that rare moment when a swinging hurley connects on impulse with an airborne sliotar. The result is a live connection, a happening, a strike such as Kennelly spoke of earlier – 'Now and then I seem to strike a line which is true and clear'. And this strike reverberates in a particular sound, a sound that is not the clichéd 'ring', but rather the '*sing*' of truth. The sing of truth in such an instant of true connection between two moving entities uplifts and divines both the player and the game at once. Such a moment is an instant of extension for the player and the game, for poetry and the poet. It surpasses even the most beautifully skilful play from a dead ball situation e.g. a sideline cut, or a free or puc-out, or the parallel graft and 'hard chaw' that goes into a poem such as:

Toffee Poetry
I bite into the hard toffee
Of my poem's unyielding
Awkwardness
In my mouth.
Can't get my tongue around this poem.
Jaws clench
Fingers tense
Words stick
In my teeth.
Pen pokes
To free the sticky toffee.

More malleable now.
I chew it over.
Mmm. I like it.
I swallow.
(Maria, 6th class)

Such an instant of connection is a metaphor for what happens when:

> the whole of the spoken language surrounding the child [and the writer] snaps him up like a whirlwind, tempts him with its internal articulations, and it is as an extension of this game that the language itself develops ... the life of language consists in the constant playing further of the game that we first learned when we began to speak.[11]

In exploring the practicalities of poetry and education thus far this book has sought to make the writing process and its inherent educational dimension more explicit. However, the various headings that punctuate this book should not be thought of as discrete competences combining to create one objective skill that can then be employed as required, or demonstrated at will. Also, while it has sought to show that poetry writing may not fit easily within current teaching practice, it agrees that:

> deep misgivings about the ascendancy of technicist theories of teaching should not be understood to imply that all teaching is good simply if it is non-technical. To the contrary, one thing I can concede to technicism is that it is an understandable response to the morass – the stale routine or sheer chaos – to which teaching can deteriorate when it is not practiced intelligently.[12]

Similarly, one's misgivings about the Greek-old urge to take control does not preclude one from acknowledging the weight of uncertainty and 'worry' that human vulnerability and contingency give rise to. Insofar as this uncertainty and attempts to deal with it are reflected in education, this thesis has sought to evidence poetry's educational role in modelling a way – not of trying to control, or escape one's 'human' nature – but of developing the skills and trust with which to negotiate in language the very heart of the matter of human experience. Working with poetry teaches, among other things, a practical humility and respect for language. Just as one cannot set out deliberately to make a poem be 'this kind of poem' or 'that kind of poem', the best one can do in writing, as in life, is 'negotiate' what happens, as it happens. At the heart of that negotiation in teaching/learning, as in writing, lies a need for aural alertness, an ongoing reflection, a capacity to address what is happening and to be addressed by it. I have no desire to add to the number of agencies – whatever their agenda – who seek to issue directives to teachers as to how and what they ought to teach. Instead, I have tried to look at and understand what education truly is. It is my belief that when poetry and education and religious education connect, centre of gravity to centre of gravity, they resound in the *sing* of an education that is true to life in all its fullness and in all its silence and in all its struggles, an education that fosters the living of a deeper life, that exemplifies kingdom-come and still coming.

By working with children's poetry I wanted to attempt two things which, like teaching and learning, practice and reflection-on-practice, are not always separable either. I wanted to *make more explicit the kind of learning that is fostered in poetry's writing process* so that it may be valued not just as an important part of the language curriculum but as an overarching model of education and religious education in itself. *At the same time* I wanted to offer some children's poems *as poetry in their own right.* This I believe is because working with poetry in the classroom is an experience of 'teaching from the boat'. Poetry's writing process is not without skill but the skill is honed in repeatedly 'putting out from the shore', trusting in 'the craft itself', that is, trusting in poetry writing as a craft that seeks 'a way' with language's shiftiness and heft, its gift of buoyancy and swim. Like the pearl of great price, poetry writing is an activity intimate with the business of seeking and finding, usually *below conscious levels of thought and feeling,* way down in language's undercurrents. Sometimes a poem is 'found' as a result of seeking; sometimes it is found without seeking. But ultimately, to use another religious metaphor, to seek a poem among the guarantees of a reliable methodology is to seek the living among the dead. Poetry and its writing process offer the opportunity to experience a way of working that is practical but not necessarily methodological, that requires discipline but is not always controllable. In doing so poetry and its writing process go to the very heart of the matter of education today. In short, if there is advice to be offered to the reader in this chapter, let me offer it now and be done with it: to engage with what the Bullock Report calls poetry's 'educative power'[13] in the classroom is pedagogically and poetically to put out from the shore, at least now and again, and play it by ear.

Notes

1. *Seeing Things,* p. 27.
2. *Preoccupations,* p. 48.
3. From Kelly, P., *Time For Poetry,* Dublin, Folens, 1991, p. 60.
4. Hughes, T., *Poetry in the Making,* London, Faber and Faber, p. 18.
5. *Back to the Rough Ground,* p. 144.
6. Ibid.
7. *Preoccupations,* p. 45.

8. *The Cox Report*, p.142.
9. *Preoccupations*, p. 47.
10. Ibid., p. 43.
11. *Back to the Rough Ground*, p. 369.
12. Ibid.
13. *A Language for Life*, Chap. 0.27, p. 137.

An Ancient Apologia

I began by saying that this book was not about proofs, arguments, objectives, outcomes, methodologies and such like. It has been the modest story of one teacher's classroom engagement with children, poetry, its writing process, and the kind of teaching and learning involved. In a way, it is my response to all the 'notes' I did not do, my alternative 'taking note' of what goes on deep down in the most primitive and primary levels of education and in myself as teacher and learner. It has been my way of coming to understand the nature of primary teaching. That teaching and learning proved to be intimately engaged with language, imagination, tradition and experience. It is an engagement that has continually attuned and re-attuned the teacher's ear to young voices in front of her, and behind them, to the ancient voices of various poets, prophets, philosophers and teachers whispering at the back of her classroom even as she continued to teach. More than anything else, it has been a process of finding a teacher voice, a voice that because it is in contact with the tradition's voices, and with present reality, has a sense of its own identity and therefore may speak with greater authority. This process of listening-in and finding a teacher voice with which to speak, as poetically as possible, the reality of my classroom experience stirs a belief in me that to become a teacher is to discover its ancestry in you. To remain a teacher is to engage that ancestry in a life-long conversation. In elaborating the learning process that poetry and its writing process sponsors, my hope for this book is that it may have done primary education both generally and religiously some modest imaginative service. 'Imagination can be recognised ... as the act of responding to a demand for new meaning, the demand of emerging realities to *be* by *being said in new ways.*'[1] I have tried to say 'education' in a new way. I have tried to respond imaginatively to what I have experienced in myself as a struggle with the role of teacher in today's educational world as I experience it. I can only now in retrospect name that struggle as the struggle of the teacher-within-me to be allowed to emerge, to bespeak herself and her reality, demanding as she does so more poetic licence for generating the meaning of what it is to be a teacher. The story told in this book is the best I can do to allow the reality of being a teacher to *be*, by being said *more poetically*.

Elizabeth Sewell has said of poets: 'They have the task of reducing the areas of human experience where language has not yet penetrated and though much here is without words it seems to struggle towards speech.'[2] In this book I have reached into education's pockets to search and find what has been struggling towards more poetic speech. I have rummaged in poetry's pockets to find what faith leads me to believe has been 'laid' there for me, so that I found it out and can now offer it modestly as food to nourish new life in others who teach and learn. Finally now, I reach into one poem in particular in order to speak poetically the process I have been engaged in throughout this book. It is a process that finds an apt objective correlative in Billy Collins' poem:

Afternoon with Irish Cows
There were a few dozen who occupied the field
across the road from where we lived,
stepping all day from tuft to tuft,
their big heads down in the soft grass,
though I would sometimes pass a window
and look out to see the field suddenly empty
as if they had taken wing, flown off to another
country.

Then later, I would open the blue front door,
and again the field would be full of their munching,
or they would be lying down
on the black and white maps of their sides,
facing in all directions, waiting for rain.
How mysterious, how patient and dumbfounded
they appeared in the long quiet afternoons.

But every once in a while, one of them
would let out a sound so phenomenal
that I would put down the paper
or the knife I was cutting an apple with
and walk across the road to the stone wall
to see which one of them was being torched
or pierced through the side with a long spear.

Yes, it sounded like pain until I could see
the noisy one, anchored there on all fours,
her neck outstretched, her bellowing head
labouring upwards as she gave voice
to the rising, full-bodied cry
that began in the darkness of her belly
and echoed up through her bowed ribs into her gaping
mouth.

Then I knew she was only announcing
the large, unadulterated cowness of herself
pouring out the ancient apologia of her kind ...
to all the green fields and the gray clouds,
to the limestone hills and the inlets of the blue bay
while she regarded my head and shoulders
above the wall with one wild, shocking eye.[3]

I am one of those 'who occupied the field' of primary education. A significant amount of what I did as the teacher of young children was informed by the experience of being a mother and daughter, i.e. of rearing and nourishing and of having been reared and nourished myself. Therefore the place where I lived was psychologically just 'across the road from where I taught'. I and my teaching kine (both women and men) are down-to-earth about what we do; 'anchored on all fours'. All day we step from tuft to tuft, heads down among the soft grass of primary curricular pastures, going from child to child, group to group, activity to activity with an innate rhythmic steadiness that measures out the days, the weeks, the terms and the generations. Sometimes I would glance through a window and see a classroom suddenly empty as if its occupants, like Collins' cows, 'had all taken wing, flown off to another country' – home perhaps, or to the land of weekends or summer holidays. Then, they're all back again and the hum of the classroom is once more a 'field full of their munching'. Occasionally, behind the 'mysterious, patient, dumbfounded *appearance*' of my teaching kine, a noisy one has erupted within me and I have bawled, 'letting out a sound so phenomenal' but painfully inarticulate also, in an effort to name that activity we call 'teaching' and give it deeper meaning.

Just as the child's hand searched her grandfather's various pockets, covering the whole course, finding things out, the poet in this poem does likewise. Interrupting proceedings with papers and peelings, the audial imagination of the poet reaches like the child's hand into the phenomenon of the cow's sound and covers a whole course of other pockets or echo-chambers – the dark belly, the echoing ribcage, the outstretched neck, the bellowing head, the gaping mouth. With the help of an audial imagination attuned by the poetry of experienced and inexperienced poets I have searched deep pockets in the ancient educational landscape – caves and swallow holes and the large watery pockets of Lough Neagh and the Sea of Galilee. Indeed every poem in this book is a pocket searched and an egg found. Collins' poem presents the valuable act of 'finding voice'. The phenomenal but inarticulate sound of the cow in question found poetic resonance that translated its bawl into poetry. What is ultimately found out or sounded out in the pages of this book is what I have been calling the teacher-voice. Poetic resonance has allowed the inarticulateness of my own bawl to pour forth – madly at times – some modest part of Teaching's ancient apologia. Poetry has helped to map the contours of education's inner pockets and echo chambers onto its outer-wordly landscape so that the unadulterated 'teacherness' of teaching may be 'Announced!', not explained or analysed or argued, but announced. Take it or leave it.

Notes

1. *Poetics of Imagining*, p. 148.
2. From 'The Death of Imagination' in Scott, N.A., *The New Orpheus: Essays Toward a Christian Poetic*, Maryland, Sheed and Ward, 1964, p. 137.
3. From *Picnic, Lightning*, Pitt Poetry Series, University of Pittsburgh Press, 1998, p. 12.